Improve Your Global Business English

To Twitter: Where random can become specific – and where this collaboration was conceived!

Heartfelt thanks to my newly-extended family (with special thanks to the dynamic young professionals in it), to all my clients, and to tweeps who have become friends, for their wonderful, valued support. We grow by sharing experiences/lessons learned, and understanding the power good communication has to build bridges and develop lasting relationships.

Special thanks to my dearest husband, Colin who is by now also an expert in word power skills!

FIONA TALBOT

To everyone who has read and reviewed my writing and to my parents, Mr and Mrs S B Mukherjee, my brother Kallol, my parents-in-law, Mr and Mrs D M Bhattacharjee and my loving husband, Sandeepan, for being so supportive.

SUDAKSHINA BHATTACHARJEE

Improve Your Global Business English

FIONA TALBOT and
SUDAKSHINA BHATTACHARJEE

KoganPage

LONDON PHILADELPHIA NEW DELHI

First published in Great Britain and the United States in 2012 by Kogan Page Limited

120 Pentonville Road	1518 Walnut Street, Suite 1100	14737/23 Ansari Road
London N1 9JN	Philadelphia PA 19102	Daryaganj
United Kingdom	USA	New Delhi 110002
www.koganpage.com		India

© Fiona Talbot and Sudakshina Bhattacharjee, 2012

ISBN   978 0 7494 6613 8
E-ISBN 978 0 7494 6615 2

British Library Cataloguing-in-Publication Data

A CIP record for this book is available from the British Library.

Library of Congress Cataloging-in-Publication Data

Talbot, Fiona.
    Improve your global business English : the essential toolkit for writing and communicating across borders / Fiona Talbot, Sudakshina Bhattacharjee.
        p. cm.
    Includes bibliographical references.
    ISBN 978-0-7494-6613-8 – ISBN 978-0-7494-6615-2   1. English language–Business English.   2. Business communication.   3. Business writing.   I. Bhattacharjee, Sudakshina.   II. Title.
    PE1479.B87T353 2012
    808.06'665–dc23   2012020912

Typeset by Graphicraft Limited, Hong Kong
Printed and bound in India by Replika Press Pvt Ltd

Contents

15 The kaleidoscope effect – further perspectives for global business English   221

You can download FREE additional checklists, templates and worksheets. Simply visit http://www.koganpage.com/editions/improve-your-global-business-english/9780749466138 and click on 'View Resources'.

Introduction

Who is the book for?

This book has been designed for go-ahead professionals who understand the need to develop quality business English communication skills in today's time-pressured, results-driven digital world.

How do you use it?

In a nutshell, we encourage you throughout 'to learn by doing'. We give tips on how to design your own customized templates using your preferred variety of English (yes, there are many!) and the right communication style for the task in hand.

So that you serve your readership well, we introduce a totally new concept, by suggesting you add your 'local splash of colour' – the 'glocal' – to make your business English right for your part of the world or the part of the world with which you are dealing.

You see, businesses need to wake up to the fact that the number of native English speakers using English worldwide is eclipsed by the number of non-native speakers using it. Both sets need to evaluate whether they are using English:

- that readers can understand, both on a linguistic and cultural level: and
- that readers can relate to personally, as well on a business level.

That's quite a challenge but we're here to help you rise to it, by offering loads of solutions! The book will quite literally open your horizons, and open your eyes to what is going on around you. You'll understand how to distinguish between successful and less successful writing styles whilst at the same time enhancing your reputation as a truly global, modern and totally professional player in today's market place.

The descriptive terminology/spelling we use

- Throughout the book when we refer to native English speakers we are referring to anyone who speaks any variety of English as their first language.

- If we need a working description of standard or global English in a business context, we suggest it is the English that displays the least regional variation and, as a result, is most widely understood globally.

- Unless we indicate otherwise, we use mid-Atlantic, not UK spelling. This means we use 'z' in organization, but don't compromise on other words such as colour or favourite – except when, in Chapter 12 we write 'favorite', the way it's expressed on Twitter. You'll find more on variant spellings later in the book.

- We use the term native English speaker/writer to mean a person whose first language is English.

- We use the term non-native speaker/writer to mean a person whose first language is not English.

- For ease of reference, we'll also sometimes use the abbreviation non-NE to refer to the non-native English speaker/writer and will refer to non-native English writing as non-NE writing.

Fiona Talbot
www.wordpowerskills.com

Sudakshina Bhattacharjee
https://sudakshinakina.wordpress.com

Chapter One
Writing English for global business

"The world may seem a smaller place; it doesn't mean we're all the same. Dialogue helps embrace the commonalities and respect the differences.

The purpose of this book

The very fact you're reading this book shows you are curious to know more about and enhance your use of global business English: the spoken and written English used as a global language in business and everyday life.

English has always been the ice-breaker language, hasn't it? Wherever you go, for example on holidays to locations outside the UK, or making that all-important business deal, English is very often the language you use, even for an initial conversation or query before going on to the details.

The purpose of this book is to help you grow your understanding and use of English in the global context of things and be aware of the cultural, social and professional environments of your readers, customers or target audience – so that you can speak, interact and write clearly, comprehensively and successfully.

We'll provide tips as building blocks to success in understanding and distinguishing between the differences in local and global English. If you use the worksheets we provide at the end of each chapter, you'll not only consolidate your learning but you'll also be able to add your 'local splash of colour' or 'seasoning to taste'. This way, you'll ensure that the business English you use is right for your target audience.

By the end of your study, you'll be more confident and competent in speaking and writing global business English, a key transferable skill that can take you places.

Defining readers, customers and target audience

We refer to readers, customers and target audience as interchangeable terms. As a professional, you need to understand the similarities and differences between these three terms.

'Reader' refers to anyone with whom you are interacting, or aiming to engage in communication. The communication could be a sales proposal letter to a potential customer, an e-mail to a colleague, and so on. We use the word 'customer' both in its most common usage as a person who buys goods or services from a business; and in the broadest sense of the word: to signify a person that you have to deal with in the course of your daily work. The term 'target audience' applies just as much to internal colleagues, to suppliers, to those in charities, or working in the public sector, as it does to external buyers or other consumers. In other words, the target audience of your company or business could be anyone who has or could potentially have an interest in your products or services.

Your audience can be anyone and everyone

We use many practical examples and scenarios throughout this book. Some relate to standard sales or pitches to customers as, whatever we do, we're all also consumers in our private lives. We all have some idea of being on the receiving end of professional and unprofessional services. Many of the topics we cover are what people traditionally understand by business writing, such as letters and reports. But largely because of the internet, writing actually dominates the business world today. It plays an ever-increasing role in scenarios you may not initially have considered as business writing. Think of the use of social media; think of lobbying, politics, charities, fundraising, promotions – to name just some examples.

The communication skills and public relations strategies applied in all these fields are crucial not only for the monetary profits of a business, but also something that's arguably just as important: its reputation. Year on year, companies are growing to understand just how precious this is, and for this reason there's an emergent new field of business: that of reputation management. In the final analysis, reputation is something that's easy to break and difficult to fix. This is particularly true with the rapid onset of social media online. So we'll show you how not to let faulty communications put your organization at risk.

Understanding cultures, subcultures and approaches to businesses and workplaces

The term 'culture' generally means a set of customs, traditions, values and conventions that are specific to a social group. Naturally where there are humans, there are differences in the way any one culture is practised, expressed and reflected. It's the same with business organizations. Each organization has its own individual way of getting work done, its own ways of communicating internally and externally. Sometimes there are even differences between or within departments that can further complicate matters. It's these intricate factors which ultimately have an impact on the level of success a business attains.

Business culture has its own set of subcultures: the further classification of processes and behaviours that make them little cultures unto themselves. There may be a reserved culture where internal communications are strongly relied upon and external communications are kept to the minimum. A reserved culture may also have different connotations based on a hierarchical belief that the individual is subordinate to the organization; that the minority is subordinate to the majority – and that the lower level is subordinate to the higher level.

You'll find this business culture prevailing in many countries, for example China and Japan. Another facet can be that the individual will do whatever it takes not to be put in a position where he or she would 'lose face'. This reserve may be linked to people not liking to embarrass colleagues by saying 'no' in a meeting and preferring to say 'yes' when they ultimately mean 'no'.

Or there can be the opposite of reserved culture, expressive culture, where openness of internal and external communications is encouraged and the individual is welcome to make his or her personal mark, as in most countries in Western Europe and in the United States. A feature of this expressive culture is the concept of empowerment, where the individual is given authority or power to authorize something. Can you see how this is a key factor to take into account when you communicate with a culture where decisions can only be taken on a collective basis?

Another feature of an expressive culture may be effusiveness, for example a US business person might state that a meeting that went well was 'truly awesome' whereas someone from a more reserved culture might comment 'that didn't go too badly'. The UK would rank as a more reserved culture in this respect even though it's in the West. An effusive business culture might expect open and constant praise when things have gone well; the reserved culture, in contrast, may sense insincerity if offered incessant praise.

There are also, of course, *informal* and *formal* cultures, where the level of expression in communication, attire, manners and courtesy vary from one organization to another. Some businesses have the subculture of focusing on relationships with their clientele. Other businesses focus on clinching deals and keeping things strictly professional and relatively impersonal – as opposed to professional with a clear personal touch.

On a slightly different point here, the proverb 'to each his own', is not limited to its socio-psychological angle. Not only does every country, city and company have shared customs and conventions, they also have their own uniqueness to distinguish them from one another. Local cultures are bound to have some effect over a company or other professional organization's work culture and its professionals. We definitely ought to identify, manage and imbibe the best bits from our local and work cultures so that our working practices and best-practice methods effectively help boost the quality of the work we do.

In recent years, some companies in the United States and the UK have taken to a more informal approach of staff working as teams, with less demarcation between the boss and his or her subordinates. The boss figure is no longer locked in an 'ivory tower', though this is still much the norm with Indian small to medium enterprises (SMEs). The general work culture there is that of respecting senior authority figures, which may even include standing up when they walk in and addressing the person as 'Sir' or 'Madam'.

We also find that bigger multinational corporations and conglomerates have followed their Western counterparts and gone open-plan. This creates scope for more open, spontaneous banter and dialogue among colleagues and with bosses.

Both conservative and open-plan approaches work because both yield results, but would a mix of approaches perhaps yield even better results? What is the approach to business in your workplace? Does your company or business blend respect to authority with casual banter among colleagues? If so, how does this affect your work environment?

This book isn't about describing all the possibilities. But we can ask you which of these cultures and subcultures best describe how your organization operates. And which best describe the cultures and subcultures with whom you communicate, if different? Also, are there specific personalities you have to deal with, within your sphere of work, that mean you have to adjust your communication further?

What to write and how much to write

Here's a question to get you thinking. At work, if you're faced with a sheet of blank white paper and you have a writing task, what do you do with that blank space?

We can tell you that when the British write for business their initial draft often fills all the white space. This is strange given that most British business readers complain about verbosity and waffle. In theory, they welcome the concept of 'plain English' which involves clear, concise messages. But counter-intuitively, they feel readers might actually feel 'short-changed' by brevity.

The British are definitely not alone: many other cultures opt for verbosity too. We've seen promotional letters two-and-a-half pages long from Indian banks to their customers – that requires staying power from readers.

Some nationalities and cultures have totally the opposite approach. When faced with that blank piece of paper, they decide that the best way forward is to leave as much white space unfilled as possible. They write short bullet points, short lists and may add a diagram. There you are, they think, the job's done. But is it? Are these writers always as efficient as they think? Do they ever realize their writing may not actually work? The real proof can be in readers' reactions and subsequent action (or inaction).

Great writing is certainly as concise as it needs to be, but it doesn't cut the intended and correct meanings out. Nor should it remove the right words to create logical connections to and for readers. Great business writers know when to amplify, with words that add value, and when to edit – to cut out verbosity. It's about understanding what needs to be expressed, rather than implied – and what's not needed at any given time.

Just because we know what our shorthand and our stark bullet points mean, it doesn't necessarily follow that our readers will too. If we fall into the trap of over-brevity, it's just as bad as the trap of verbosity. In both cases, we take our readers into 'a world of customer disservice'. Readers of different nationalities won't thank us for it.

To demonstrate, let's compare two rather extreme styles of writing.

Example 1

The head of department reported that the additional, unexpectedly inflated, expenditure on office stationery, arising from the company's rebranding exercise, could not be met from current reserves and that, although he might have to ask staff to make savings, it did appear that the expenditure could be accommodated by putting an embargo on any managers undertaking any first-class travel in December.

The length of the sentence and the number of commas needed shows that the sentence needs editing. In this first example, all the reader really needs to know is:

- There is additional, unexpected expenditure that cannot be met from current reserves.
- A ban on first-class travel in December would recoup this amount.
- If the ban does not recoup the amount, staff might have to be asked to make savings.

Example 2

- Absenteeism;
- Stocking shelves;
- Waste.

In the second example, only the writer can know what he or she means in this bullet point list. Even if it's going to be explained face to face at some stage, this writing is never going to be meaningful by itself. Yet just a small amount of reworking would make its meaning clear. For example, maybe 'Absenteeism' in the first bullet point refers to: 'Problem of absenteeism: what are the root causes?' The subject immediately becomes more accessible. It means more to readers, even before it is discussed.

Which of the two examples is your style closer to? Is either extreme ideal? When you write for global business it's generally going to work better to go for a middle path. Develop a style that certainly edits down to the main points (cutting out waffle) but also includes enough information, so every message is entire and meaningful. It's crucial you do this. Writing is a medium that's likely to be read when you are not there to explain it – and that may also be relayed to recipients of whom you may be unaware. It's foolish to ignore this.

Regardless of how experienced we are, when it comes to writing that all-important letter or e-mail, we should think, and then think some more. It's not a bad thing to be a bit apprehensive about the response we may get. Let's face it, interaction is crucial and we need it to be as positive as possible. Managers don't encourage a care-free attitude in business performance generally, so why should they view writing any differently?

It can help readers to know, in the broadest terms, what a particular non-native English speaker's background is. That writer's choice of words and the way he or she writes is likely to reflect this. Armed with some awareness of this, readers are more likely to allow some leeway in interpretation – and be more tolerant. It can make all the difference – and offer 'Eureka moments,' where readers see why the writer wrote that way: 'Oh, that's why she wrote that! Now I understand her viewpoint.'

Let's use examples from Dutch-English to illustrate this point. To put things in perspective, the Dutch can be some of the best business English writers in the world. A proud nation of traders, they accept that Dutch isn't a global language and they need to master other languages to succeed in international markets. Yet even they routinely make the same mistakes when they write in English. Although they may be small mistakes, they can confuse native and non-native English readers unaccustomed to these idiosyncrasies. Here are some examples.

The translation of the English word 'or' is 'of' in Dutch. So Dutch-English will regularly include errors such as 'Either you of Gert could go to the meeting.' (Correct English is 'Either you or Gert could go to the meeting.')

Another common mistake is to confuse the English 'either... or' for 'or... or'. For example: 'Or we go to London or we go to Paris.' (Correct English is 'Either we go to London or we go to Paris'.)

These errors seem minor but they can make life difficult for readers. If, however, readers have fore-knowledge that these are errors that the Dutch (as one example) often make, readers then make allowances – and more easily understand the intended meaning.

Understanding personality alongside culture can also be helpful. Some personalities tend to write complicated long sentences or produce unstructured writing that takes readers all over the place – but not necessarily where they want to be. On the other hand, those who are overly economical with their words can come across as so terse that hardly anything is communicated at all. Neither extreme is ideal. What's better is to relay essential communication (of key points and important information) in a personable and appropriate manner.

It's really helpful to know writers' backgrounds because then readers may be:

- less offended by extremely direct exchanges;
- less puzzled if people don't appear willing to take the lead on decisions;
- less frustrated by hierarchical language where a writer will only deal with a chief executive or senior manager directly;
- less impatient when they understand the person with whom they are communicating has to seek the consensus of others, before he or she can reply to any request;
- less bemused by overly polite language.

The three Ss – smart, sophisticated and successful

Today's job markets are becoming less restricted to basing locations in one place from where all the work happens. Modern working life has gone global, requiring professionals to be **smart** in their presentation, **sophisticated** in their style and dealings, and to exude the confidence and 'oomph' that comes with being **successful**.

Smart, **sophisticated** and **successful** are what we call the three Ss, but what do they really mean? Here we'll look at them in turn. Where they are discussed later, we have picked them out in bold type as a reminder that we are using them with the specific meanings given below.

Smart

The word 'smart' means different things to different people. In the United States 'a smart person' often means someone who knows a lot. In the UK it can mean that, and it may also mean the person is dapper and stylish. What does it mean to you?

In this book, we define **smart** as not just about being great in what you do in your daily performance; it is also about really understanding your role and its importance in the grand scheme of things (the company or business infrastructure). Additionally, it's about you valuing your personal effort in your work.

Ask yourself whether you actively do these things. Your answers will help you realize where you, as a skilled professional, stand in your workplace and the industry you're in. This knowledge, in turn, will give you an inner power that enables you to spur your career onwards and upwards. This is what being **smart** is all about.

Sophisticated

The word 'sophisticated' has clear connotations for most. It's about being aware of and able to interpret complex issues. It's also about showing worldly experience of fashion and culture.

We won't be using it here to cover fashion, except as a metaphor. We believe that words are the clothes for our logic – and we believe individuals have to choose the right words for the business task in hand and for the cultural sensibilities they encounter. This helps you see what we mean by **sophisticated** in this section. In accessible language, we could suggest you wouldn't go to a formal business black-tie event in jeans, would you? So clothe your logic in words that do you and your readers justice – certainly not the bare minimum.

We're also noticing that people worldwide react positively to elegance of expression, so that's another meaning we attach to **sophisticated** in a communication context.

The rise in globalization has left in its wake countless multinational companies who have headquarters in one place, manufacturing sites in other places and trade destinations dotted across the globe. Judgements are always made on whether you are **sophisticated** enough, in the other sense of the word, to show worldly experience of the culture and other issues affecting your audience. Whether you're speaking publicly or privately, or you're just an observer, the way you come across to other professionals carries a great deal of importance.

This rise in globalization has, in turn, brought new concepts, like going 'glocal', where global and local cultures merge to ensure that mutual respect and understanding prevail all around. In case you haven't heard the term 'glocal' before, it was coined in the United States from a phrase 'think global, act local', adopted for the social justice movement.

Time and time again companies learn (sometimes the hard way) that if people don't feel respected, they feel disinterested or even worse, offended. This can translate into loss of business. So, to be

sophisticated is not just to have good manners, but an assured aura which gives off signals that you and your company or business have credibility.

It's about truly believing in yourself, your capabilities and aptitudes, as well as being an ambassador for your business. If you don't believe in the work that you or your organization does, you'll have less esteem and regard for where your company stands. This won't give off secure and confident cues to the outside world. What's more, if you deliver this **sophisticated** aura, not only does your commitment in doing this help people believe in and respect you, but also they're likely to believe that you understand and respect them.

Successful

Being successful is an easy concept to understand, but how easy is it to be successful? It does actually rather depend upon on your own perception: what does being successful mean to you personally and/or in your work? Does it mean leading a glamorous life with high status? Does it mean getting things done with minimal fuss? Is it linked to profits and material gain? Does it mean creating a highly visible profile with a wide-spreading business empire and lots of employees? Or does it mean keeping your head down and getting on with the work, calmly, quietly, steadily? Does it mean a mixture of all the above? Any of these could of course be the right answer; it just depends on the context: only you can provide the answer.

To us though, for the purpose of this book, being **successful** is to do work that brings prospects for further growth and that ultimately benefits yourself and any organization you work for (and with). Last but certainly not least, being successful is about positive audience engagement and ongoing interaction, for mutual benefit.

The three Cs – clear, comprehensible and confident

To achieve the three Ss your use of global business English should have the three Cs – it should be clear, comprehensible and confident. This is where knowing how to use the right business English comes in. Here are our definitions, and where these terms appear here and in later chapters, they are typeset in bold as a visual reminder.

Clear

We all understand the concept of being clear: sending unambiguous messages that people should find easy to understand. But in a global context we need to factor in that the perception of clarity may vary from reader to reader. Do we use our local idiom when writing to someone not from our locality? Or should we use readily understood global English?

Many major corporations strike a balance between both. They know when they need to come across as a global entity – and when to add that splash of local colour that makes all the difference in making their customers feel at home.

It probably won't take long before this trend becomes a convention in today's world of modern business communications. It's crucial because if you don't use the right words coupled with the right tone, you won't strike the right chord with the people you are doing business with.

So, being **clear** is a hugely important factor. There's no room for compromise, yet many companies overlook this. We'll be giving more practical help regarding clear communication in Chapter 9.

Comprehensible

If the communication that you send is clear, then it's more likely it will be **comprehensible** (understandable for the receivers). It's really about checking that what is clear to you can actually be understood by them. An all too common mistake is to make what might otherwise have been clear writing incomprehensible – for example, by the use of obscure jargon (see also Chapter 9).

If your readers can comprehend your meaning, it's much easier for them to do any further analysis and any other follow-on activities in order to make good business decisions. Negotiations, to take just one example, can be seriously hampered by misunderstandings. Or business deals may even be lost – all because someone, somewhere, failed to understand all, or even just one part, of a message.

It follows that the more **comprehensible** you are, the better your business communications will be. And being **clear** and **comprehensible** should go hand in hand (though we cannot assume that they do).

Confident

Confidence is something you need to have in order to communicate clearly and comprehensively, as well as to deal well with any communication you receive. Being **confident** is directly related to being smart and sophisticated in that you need to have faith in your abilities and aspirations to take you further. If every individual in a business organization topped up his or her confidence imagine the strong positive force this could create – to help the organization surge forward and take the business to new heights.

To summarize, the achievable ideal is that your communication is **clear** so you identify key, unambiguous messages, is **comprehensible** so readers understand and can make informed decisions, and gives off a strong sense of being **confident** in the manner in which the communication is expressed.

Worksheet

Section A: Knowing your theory

Based on what you have understood from this chapter, indicate whether or not you agree with the following statements by ticking the 'Yes' or 'No' boxes.

		Yes	No
1	In a global business context, empathy means having an awareness of the cultural, linguistic and professional environments of your readers, customers or target audience.	☐	☐
2	Reputation management is an emerging field in the world of global business communications.	☐	☐

	Yes	No
3 The opposite of a reserved culture is an expressive culture, where professionals are encouraged to be open and creative in the ways they communicate.	☐	☐
4 If your customer base knows a bit about you, customers are likely to feel less offended when you are direct with them and less bothered if you are overly polite.	☐	☐
5 To be **smart** is to know your stuff and believe in the value you are adding.	☐	☐
6 To be **sophisticated** is to put people off with a know-it-all attitude.	☐	☐
7 To be **clear** is to make sure what you say and write identifies key points well.	☐	☐
8 Jargon can make clear writing incomprehensible, which means others may not understand it.	☐	☐

Section B: Approaching the white space

Let's go back to the question we asked you earlier on in this chapter. At work, if you are faced with a sheet of blank white paper and you have a writing task, what do you do with that blank space? Would you fill it up from corner to corner? Would you keep things very brief? Or would you try to strike a balance between verbosity and brevity in the document?

How would you introduce your company to potential customers? Imagine the empty box below is going to become a letter you have to send en masse, informing your target audience about the products and services your company offers and how these would benefit them. Try writing this letter and then review it critically, in the light of all the points made in this first chapter. If you need some tips on structuring letters this topic is covered in Chapter 5.

Chapter Two
Why do we write in business?

> *Design your business communication to work so that you get the results you need.*

Writing is a soft skill but not a soft option

In business, communication is often classified as a 'soft skill'. This has always seemed a misnomer to us, as it wrongly seems to suggest that it is a soft option – something that comes easily to most people, either on the sending or receiving end. It's probably for this reason that few companies offer anything like adequate training in this crucial management tool.

Business writing is just one aspect of business communication. But in fact it's probably the key driver in the world of business and commerce today. Face-to-face communication is on the decrease globally, thanks to the relentless rise of the internet. Business telephone calls are scarcer by the day. Without a shadow of a doubt, it is e-mails and instant messaging (both as internal and external communications) that predominate in today's technology-driven business world.

But is writing really an easy medium to master? And we do mean master, not simply to 'have a go at'. Because isn't business writing also one of the most unforgiving forms of communication imaginable? The written word has always had to say what you mean it to say if it's to succeed. Now, thanks to the internet, we also expect most of what we read to get to the point speedily. If we have something to write (and let's face it, we're almost all business writers today), then the speed factor presents an extra hazard to negotiate. The minute you've ever had to say 'Oh, I never meant to say that!' (and who hasn't?) is the minute you'll know exactly what we mean.

Throughout the book we show how there's a price tag for every piece of ineffective business writing we send out. If we get it wrong we can be ignored, or we can impede performance (our own or others' or both). Or there can be other costly outcomes such as loss to other rival companies, simply because they have delivered better. It doesn't stop there: ineffective writing can come back to haunt us in other ways such as by prompting complaints – or when we find we've blocked our promotion prospects by being noticed for the wrong reasons.

We ignore our business writing skills at our peril. It's largely because readers often make instant decisions about our professional competence on the basis of our workplace writing. It can take just a couple of seconds for potential readers to decide whether or not they will read what you've written. Unless you're writing a document they have to use, you don't have the ultimate power here: your readers do! You'll know that in your own experience as a consumer.

Having chosen to read this book is testimony to the fact that you know it takes real skill (and some hard graft) if your writing is:

- for a start, to be read;
- to be understood correctly;
- to reflect your professionalism;
- to be seen to say what you mean it to say.

If you manage to engage your readers to the extent they read your writing, then it's likely that 'what they see is what they think they'll get'. Unless you're physically with your audience, face to face or voice to voice to explain your message, everything depends on how you expressed yourself at the moment of writing.

What a shame (and that's probably an understatement) that so many written messages lead to confusion and misunderstanding – even when people are writing in their native language. Many lead to customer complaints. Can it ever be worth the risk?

Even if companies pat themselves on the back by converting complaints into an ultimately positive experience (perhaps by appropriate follow-up action to sort out the issues), it has probably doubled the time, money and effort involved in the original writing task. And that's not an end to it. Customers are likely to tell others about the bad experience they have either received or think they have received. In the worst scenarios, they'll walk away from the 'offending' company.

That's the commercial effect that ineffective writing can have. We all know that if, as customers, we don't understand or like what supplier A is writing, it can be our preferred option to buy from supplier B, who cares enough about our time and our needs to get the message right. And if this is in shorter time, how much the better!

It means that, at the very least, each time you write, you need to think, write, check your meaning, spelling and grammar. Only then are you really ready to send out your writing, if you truly want your words to work for and not against you. It's a demanding task. There are no short cuts to quality.

An outline of the history of English

English is a hybrid language, first formed from language spoken by tribes in Denmark and Northern Germany who settled in Britain in the fifth and sixth centuries. Modern English includes many words of Anglo-Saxon origin (such as 'boat', 'Thursday') – and words derived from languages as diverse as Latin ('lingua franca'), Greek ('tragedy'), Celtic ('crag'), Dutch ('waffle'), French ('justice'), Arabic ('algebra') and Indian ('bungalow'). That's just to mention a few.

Of course all languages evolve: it's just that English soaks up more influences than many. It's a flexible language with a fairly simple grammar, though plenty of irregularities. What's more, there are often different ways of being right. We can choose to write judgment or judgement, customise or customize and UK spellcheck in Microsoft Word (as an example) will certainly allow us both options.

This book isn't a language primer but it's helpful for you to know there are some differences in style that are contentious even among native English speakers. Forewarned is forearmed, as we say. As an example, some just don't accept it's ever correct to split the infinitive. As you may hear this at your workplace, let's explain.

> The infinitive of a verb in English is the basic form from which most other parts of most verbs can be formed, for example 'to act'.
>
> If we want to add an adverb (to modify the verb) some traditionalists would, for example, write:
>
> To act quickly will prevent problems.
>
> But very many writers (and this includes native as well as non-native English speakers) don't agree with this (or don't know what a split infinitive is) and will write:
>
> To quickly act will prevent problems.

What do we suggest? Well, in this book we try to avoid split infinitives, not because we disapprove of them but because we know some readers really don't appreciate them. If you can avoid a problem, do so. It's a pragmatic business principle.

Another point you may hear is that English sentences mustn't end with a preposition (a word showing the relationship between one thing and another) such as 'for' or 'with'. People who believe this argue that you shouldn't, for example, write: 'It's a nice company to do business with.' They would suggest the correct form is: 'It's a nice company with which to do business.'

We have to say that in this book you will find some sentences that end with prepositions. Sometimes to avoid this can sound overly formal (even contrived) in today's business world. Rest assured though, this book is absolutely not about getting into academic discussions, interesting as they are. Its aim is simpler: to offer practical help for communicating in accessible language, so you find it easy to communicate with, and be understood by, your target business audience.

Sometimes all you need to do is look and listen: identify what is best practice for you. See what pleases those in your audience and where you can adapt your style to suit and serve them best.

What is standard and variant English?

It's easy to define business English. It's quite simply the name given to the English used for dealing with business communication in English. But if we look for definitions of standard English or variant English it's quite hard to find an easy answer. English has no regulating body or academy (such as in France) set up to preserve the language's purity. As we've seen, English owes its very existence to its ability to assimilate, even welcome loanwords (new vocabulary from other countries) into its own lexis.

If we need a working description of standard or global English for the purpose of this business-oriented book, we suggest it is the English that displays the least regional variation. As a result, this is the English most widely understood globally.

If we widen the description to talk about standard UK English or about standard US English, these standard forms are the ones taught in schools and the varieties most in use professionally in these countries or where standard English is taught worldwide. In this book we write in standard UK English unless we state otherwise.

Variant English, on the other hand, is easier to define: in this book it's all other varieties of English used. And what's really interesting is that variant English dominates worldwide.

How many people use English across the globe? Well, a few years ago, the UK government estimated more than a billion people speak English and that, by 2020, two billion people worldwide will be learning or teaching the language. It's clear that English no longer simply belongs to the nation that gives it its name. In fact it belongs to no single culture – which actually gives it a competitive edge, in that there's a ready global market of people for whom (at first sight at least) it offers mutual intelligibility across borders and cultures.

But if people don't understand how to use English as common currency, it can actually create barriers to understanding. We have seen this on numerous occasions in meetings, for example. Have you?

Often it's because non-native speakers use English in unconventional ways. Or it might be that a native UK English speaker is using English in a different way than a US English speaker. There is a witticism that Britain and the United States 'are divided by a common language'. Naturally, both countries think their version is the better.

So yes, it's important to realize UK English is not exactly the same as the many further variations of business English that exist, some of which we list later. The trouble is there's no getting away from the fact that business communication is crucial to success. If people are puzzled by it, it's seriously bad news. We can't pretend it doesn't matter because it does. Getting the right messages out and receiving the right answers back is the lifeblood of commercial success.

That's why we've explained in the introduction the writing convention we use. It makes it clear to readers from the outset. We suggest you decide which convention you'll use, to avoid unfounded or unnecessary criticism by others. Because one thing is sure: if people can find grounds for criticizing writing, they will. We warned you that it's not a soft option. Be prepared and, if asked, be able to name not only which variant you are using – but also why. Knowledge is power!

Try to be consistent, because consistency in approach underpins a strong, quality-conscious corporate image. You may undermine this if people in your company mix and match UK English spell and grammar check with US English, for example in internal communications. This happens all the time, often without people realizing.

English: A global language but is it a global currency?

Just because English appears at a glance to be a global business currency doesn't always mean it really is 'common currency'. In this book you'll often see that global business English is a mixture of global and local varieties (in a sense the glocal we referred to in Chapter 1).

The picture is quite complex. As well as different varieties of English, there are sub-varieties directly caused by mixing English with the language patterns of the native country. Examples are Chinese English, Indian English, Hindi English, Singapore English and Malaysian English – and the phenomenon can happen in any language mix.

Here are some examples in business use:

- *'Can or not?'* in Singapore English means 'Is this possible?' in standard English.

- '*I very like this*' in Chinese English means 'I like this very much' in standard English;

- '*Our offices can be availed in central Kolkata*' in Indian English; 'can be availed in' means '*can be found in*' or '*are situated in*', in standard English.

Some instances are easy enough to understand if you're from outside the user group; some are not. And some countries' governments react to the challenge such language mixes pose, in the interest of promoting international business.

CASE STUDY 2008 Beijing Olympics

During the planning stage for the 2008 Beijing Olympics, the authorities in China realized that written Chinese English could sometimes cause confusion.

Anticipating a huge influx of foreign visitors, they realized that mistranslations appeared not just in signage in public places where visitors would go but also on tourist menus, and so on. They also saw the commercial importance of ensuring the correctness of anything written in English for sale at the time, or for future export (for example labels on products or instruction leaflets).

As one municipal spokesman acknowledged, 'misinformation had become a headache for foreigners.' Thus the Chinese people were asked to look afresh at the business English writing that was needed. Feedback was requested for suggestions on how to get it right: an extremely positive reaction to solving the problem.

In another assessment, the Singapore government discouraged the use of the popular form of Singapore English called Singlish, in favour of Singapore standard English. Though many feel Singlish is a valid marker of Singaporean identity, the government believe a standard English improves Singaporeans' ability to communicate effectively with other English users throughout the world.

Problems can arise when taking a global perspective too. Even taking a small sample of anglicized words used in Western Europe, similar problems sometimes appear. We see words such as in the context of parking (in UK English: a 'car park', in US English: a 'parking lot'); the term 'presentation charts' is used predominantly in Germany (in UK English and US English: presentation 'slides') or the word 'handy' in continental Europe (in UK English: 'mobile phone'; in US English 'cell phone'; in Malaysian English: 'handphone') or 'beamer' in France and elsewhere (in UK English: 'projector'). But if we're writing globally, by definition we have to realize that we are not just writing for readers in one country.

Let's look again at that word 'charts' used by many German companies for presentation slides. To a native English reader, the word 'charts' means graphs or tables. If someone writes that he or she is preparing charts to include in a presentation, then e-mails slides without any graphs or tables, what might the reader assume? Very probably that the presentation is incomplete. Then valuable time may be lost before the reader e-mails or telephones the sender, to ask 'When am I going to receive the "missing" items, please?' The person's tone might be less polite when he or she realizes that the delay was caused by one word, used in a 'glocal' not global sense.

Take also the example of the word 'handy' for a mobile phone or 'beamer' for projector. Most native English speakers are unlikely to have any idea what these words mean in this context. So define the terms you use for your global audience as far as you possibly can.

And do periodically check understanding, whoever you deal with. This is especially important where people come from cultures where they might feel they lose face by having to ask what you mean.

Defining global business English within your organization

It can be a really useful exercise to carry out some sort of survey, to evaluate if the terms you use really are understood by your target audience. Have you ever stopped to do this?

You could draw up a formal audit or simply capture points via a brainstorming exercise. It's an obvious exercise, yet rarely done. We don't understand why not – as terms that are understood in the West may not have the same currency in the East, just as one example. Just because words and expressions sound English (and that's often all it is) this doesn't mean the words are internationally recognized.

If you work in an organization, it's really useful to share your findings with colleagues. That way you can get consensus on how to define the business English you plan to use in your global marketplace.

Managers who lead cross-cultural teams often comment on how differently team members may approach their writing. Part of the reason is clearly that cultures start out from slightly different (or even very different) perspectives. Much will additionally depend on national teaching curricula. Also, teachers may even teach English (or at least some aspects of it) wrongly, then it can become hard for learners to break bad habits. Even if not taught wrongly, some nationalities are taught rather old-fashioned styles of English that need adapting for today's business writing.

But it's never going to be enough simply to note the differences, as these can unintentionally divide the very teams that are meant (and very importantly, want) to be pulling together. You'll manage the task far better if you draw up guidelines:

- to foster some consistency in corporate approach;
- to help develop effective working relationships in your cross-cultural teams;
- to be issued in any induction programme your company may operate, either now or in the future.

Using office guidelines and in-house style

Itemize all aspects of what you write in English

This brings us back to the question at the start: why do you write in business? Can you itemize all aspects of your writing? It would help you greatly so that you don't look at things in isolation.

It then helps you assess whether you have – or should have – a house style for each writing task. If not, is this something your organization should be looking at? Corporate strategy and operations have to join up, don't they? So why not communication: the very management tool that's supposed to bring everything together? When it does, companies, readers, customers and target audience can reap the benefits, such as:

- seeing a consistent, quality professional image;
- appreciating seamless communication (rather than the disjointed writing that's the norm for many companies);
- removing from the equation the often all too apparent divisiveness (even open competition) between departments!

Lead by example

Your writing should lead by example. If you do have a house writing style, make sure you publicize it. Ensure that everybody knows it and uses it for each writing task.

Don't forget, you have to stick to the code too. Staff buy-in better when managers practise what they preach, don't they? It's a fact that staff always scrutinize their managers' writing. They too look for evidence of best practice. After all, how can you ask people to follow if you don't show the best way – in *all* you do?

Checklist of things to consider

You should consider:

- physical aspects such as font, point size and layout, punctuation, when to use capital letters, date and time conventions, etc;
- how to convey openness and honesty;
- conveying other company values too;
- how to sell company messages;
- how to produce writing that is results-focused and sent at the right time to the right people;
- using writing styles that are concise – but not at the cost of not saying the right things;
- the tone for the target sector.

The checklist isn't a final list, though you'll be getting the idea of the type of things that can be involved. Here are more tips to help you:

- Don't stop at defining house style and printing guides as hard copy.
- Post these on the intranet if appropriate.
- Update regularly, as business moves on.
- Cascade any changes through the organization.

Designate a style champion

It can be good to have a global business English style champion. If you cannot do this yourself, designate someone if you can to promote style guidelines. Get your English right every time. Companies routinely designate champions to promote individual initiatives. Why act differently about the key skill of written communication? There's virtually no cost involved in harnessing written word power effectively. But it will save you money through improved performance.

Worksheet

Section A: Knowing your theory

Based on what you have understood from this chapter, respond to the following statements by ticking the 'Yes' or 'No' boxes.

		Yes	No
1	It is assumed that communication comes easily to most people and is therefore regarded to be a 'soft skill' and also a soft option.	☐	☐
2	When they see our business writing, readers make judgements about our professional competence.	☐	☐
3	There is just one variety of English.	☐	☐
4	Ineffective or faulty writing can come back to haunt us in the form of complaints, or of no responses where we needed them.	☐	☐
5	Spelling and grammar checkers help to assure quality.	☐	☐
6	'Glocal' has the same meaning as 'global'.	☐	☐
7	The corporate image of your company will be affected if you are inconsistent in your communications.	☐	☐
8	An in-house style guide will only work when both staff and managers follow it for best practice.	☐	☐

Section B: Styling your business communications

In this chapter, we looked at the importance of creating and using in-house style guides. Does your company or business have one? If yes, how have you been asked to use it? If no, can you find out why there isn't one?

Meanwhile, in the box below, have a go at creating an in-house style guide for your company or business. Use the criteria in the box to help you.

Your company name:

Document: In-house style guide

Part 1: General editing style

Consider which variety of English to use (this will affect your spelling and grammar check), punctuation, units of measurement, font (including italic and bold features), URLs in text, computing terms, currency units, dates, etc.

Also think about page layout (margins, line spacing etc), font size, headers and footers, page numbering, etc.

Part 2: Company vision and values

Consider how to communicate these in written communications.

Part 3: Dealing with other sources

Consider use of electronic submission of discs, tables, artwork, appendices, indexes, references, permissions, commercial products, etc.

Part 4: Industry-specific styles

Consider how to use terminology that is specific to the industry to which your company or business belongs. If readers may see terminology as jargon or otherwise difficult to understand, consider using a glossary of acceptable terms and abbreviations. (This can be particularly useful in cross-cultural communication generally.)

Part 5: Confidentiality and classification

Any company needs to have a generally understood approach to the classification of documents, for example 'commercially sensitive', 'confidential', 'highly confidential', and how to mark and manage such categories of information. Increasingly, companies also implement specific e-mail policies (see Chapter 6).

Chapter Three
Deciding your business writing objectives in the digital age

> *You have the power to choose the words you write, so choose the right ones. And yes, this applies to the workplace too. Make a difference!*

The changing face of writing in the digital age

We live in the information age, which can sometimes be in danger of becoming the 'information overload' age. As never before, we want – and expect – to access facts and figures almost immediately. Why? It's probably because mostly we gather information (sometimes mistaken for knowledge) at the click of a button. This is the time of the 'digital economy', an expression to describe when people, communications infrastructures and ever-developing technology come together to provide a global platform for trade, social and other interactions.

Naturally culture comes into the equation, as people react differently to the new technology. Some cultures accept it full-on. For some, every-thing has to be geared towards the present. Theirs is the 'I-want-it-and-I-want-it-right-now' mentality. Others will have in-built slowing-down mechanisms. For example, they will agree that new solutions may well be needed, but tomorrow will do.

Maybe this example will help you define your take on this. Let's say you need someone to install a connection to the internet. Do you expect this to be in place in 2–3 days or 2–3 weeks? A Spanish businessman helpfully passed on this example, to paint a picture of different cultures' expectations, according to his experience. He labelled the first expectation the Anglo-Saxon mindset and the second the South American approach. As he deals with both mind-sets at work, labelling expectations in this way helps him design communication that works. We understand exactly what he means. In this book, we don't plan to label stereotypes but we do paint scenarios to help you realize how many global perspectives there are to take into account. So we'll ask you questions such as: will today do to perform a particular task? Or should it have been done yesterday? Or would you accept the open-ended mañana (literally tomorrow in Spanish – but which may, in the event, not even be the day after tomorrow)? Or does a deadline of 'right now' actually mean right now for you? It certainly does in most corporate sectors in the UK, the United States and India, and increasingly in the UAE we are told, to mention just a very few examples. Or maybe your viewpoint changes according to the circumstances.

The plan is that you customize your own guidelines to help you, taking into account the fact that expectations will vary from culture to culture. But there are some universal truths. For instance, we can say that the speed and exuberance of the information age can make us all feel as if the world in general, and the world of business in particular, would not work without it.

Harnessing the power of the written word, not just in paper documentation but in electronic communications as well, can turn even relatively junior members of staff in an organization into masters of multitasking! In the past, it may have seemed a superhuman task to juggle five projects at a time – but the digital age means that probably most employees have, let's say, 20 or so work tasks going on simultaneously.

How is this possible? It's largely because electronic tools help us organize our tasks and our administration. If you need to travel on business, there's a tool to let you book your e-ticket; there's a tool to let you organize your diary and your colleagues' diaries too; another to prioritize your tasks, and so on.

Electronic business writing, for example in e-mails, on websites or in social networking media, allows you the opportunity and the bonus to juggle it all yourself. Beyond that, you can expand your messages with sound, videos or other images in ways that you couldn't in the paper age. But you have to understand *how* to write digitally – the tools don't teach you that.

It's about sending written messages that are understood at a glance and that need constant updating, as they seem to become 'history immediately'. Hyperlinks may be great in encouraging brevity and cross-referencing in a more **sophisticated** and almost limitless way than was ever possible in the paper age. But hyperlinks won't work if you don't include connectors to explain to readers why the link is there.

Yet how many times have you seen a link 'cut and pasted' – dropped in without explanation by a thoughtless writer who doesn't care about helping readers navigate the information? Also remember that hyperlinks can break – or the target you want to hit goes missing – so you need to review them periodically, to check they still work.

If you are creating website content from scratch – a specialized subject, not covered in detail in this book – there are constantly changing trends which you need to stay abreast of. But the underlying and enduring features of writing for websites include:

- navigability around the various content on the site;
- at-a-glance interest and clarity;
- being **comprehensible** in a potentially global context;
- the use of keywords and expressions to enable search engines to locate the content you have written.

We'll discuss writing for established websites further in Chapter 11.

Do be careful when you write in the digital age not to immerse yourself in a world without personal interaction. Don't create a wave of information overload to drown both you and your audience. That's why we show you later in this chapter (and in Chapter 7) how, in this world where almost everyone can do everything, it's through your ideas that you can make a difference. Set them in writing and set yourself apart by the right impact. Be extra careful not to make mistakes, as the digital world magnifies them. They often can't be retrieved and corrected – and, worse still, they can go viral!

We'll be giving you tips on writing global business English electronically in Chapters 6 and 12. In the meantime, it's a useful exercise to give some thought as to how you see the difference between writing business e-mails and business letters, which are still common in various parts of the world, and for some specific purposes.

What might the differences be? First, some say a business letter should ideally not be more than one side of an A4 sheet, whereas e-mails, while generally concise and to the point, can be longer if necessary. Indeed, it's rather amusing that people don't seem to object to long business e-mails in the same way as they object to long business letters!

Second, we can embed hyperlinks to audio, image and PDFs in e-mails. It makes sending work much more convenient; with letters we need to enclose documents, CDs, etc which can take days (even weeks) in the post – and which costs more.

Third, there is the obvious factor of time and immediacy. We can send, receive and reply to e-mails as soon as possible, anywhere in the world, as long as we have an internet connection. We don't need a laptop or desktop PC either, thanks to the advent of smartphones and tablet devices.

Activity

What other advantages do you think business e-mails have over business letters? List them here – as well as situations where letters may be considered more appropriate in your particular business culture.

_____

_____

_____

_____

_____

_____

Describing what you and your organization do

For the world at large, successful business communication isn't just about output. It's about results. And you'll be hampered in getting the right results if you cannot, at the very outset, describe what you and your organization do. You actually let yourself down if:

- you fumble for words when asked what you do;
- you allow yourself to be a commodity, maybe even on 'autopilot', when you send a piece of writing out;
- you don't seize the opportunity to make an impact, perhaps even a pitch in your communication whenever you can, even if you're not actively selling.

Here's a method to help you focus on defining and describing your message:

1 You absolutely need to know what you do in order to describe what you do.

2 You need to be able to describe this within the framework of what your organization does.

3 You must identify what you need to achieve each time you write.

It's a common sense approach but people don't always think it through. So the next step is to ask yourself: why am I writing global English? The usual answers we receive are:

- to inform or record;
- to seek information;
- to write specifications;
- to achieve a standard;
- to write reports.

People often stop there. But why? There are some glaring omissions, aren't there? Can you think of any? After considerable prompting, we generally find people come up with these suggestions:

- to persuade;
- to promote services;
- to engage interest and involve;

- to get the right results;
- to sell;
- to support customers;
- to improve life for customers;
- to eat, breathe and live our vision.

Now we're into interesting territory: the lifeblood of business. So why do people often need prompting so that they come up with these vital aims? Those in truly proactive organizations shouldn't need prodding to get to the real point, should they?

Interestingly and really encouragingly, the observation 'to eat, breathe and live our vision' was made by a relatively junior employee working for a charity. She attended an open workshop where the majority of delegates were from the private sector. She made the point with such sincerity and such conviction, she absolutely wowed everyone. That's what passionate word power blended with integrity can do. People sense there's nothing 'over the top' or false about it.

So, we put this question to you. Surely words that inspire – in the literal sense of 'breathing life into something or someone' – should be uppermost in our minds when we write? They shouldn't be hidden in the backs of our minds, only emerging when our audience work hard to get answers from us, should they?

In Chapter 8 there's a system to help you structure your global business English writing. But it won't work as well as it should if you don't first look at where *you* fit into the picture.

Focus on the message, not just the translation

Most readers say they prefer clear business writing. Quite bizarrely, the moment many start to write is the moment they start to embellish their writing. Intuitively they feel that 'clear is good' – but almost feel pressurized to write unclear English. They seem to worry that if they write as they speak, they might be too clear! So it is that, sadly, even the most articulate speakers can become the most convoluted writers. Their messages can become obscured by verbosity, or waffle as it's sometimes called.

Can writing that's easy to read really impress? This concern applies to native and non-native English writers alike, though there can also be cultural influences, as we discuss throughout. There's definitely an added complication for non-native writers who may be anxious about personal failure when they write business English.

This is why we find some people translating their language into English, on a word-for-word basis. The irony is that focusing on translating single components can make non-native English writers lose sight of the intrinsic business message itself. The meaning behind each word is often more important than the literal word itself. Furthermore, the overall meaning may not be the sum of each individual word. There may be an added complication by the knock-on effect that even one wrongly chosen word can have.

We often see an over-embellished written sentence such as:

There is a requirement that a hard hat must be placed on one's head when one enters the location.

When spoken, the sentence would more likely be:

When on site, you must wear a hard hat at all times for your safety.

So something got lost, not just in translation but also in the act of writing, and that something was the crucial element of safety.

There's no doubt that you can lose sight of your objectives if your message becomes subordinate to or even eclipsed by the translation. It's commercial folly. So keep your eye on what your writing should be saying to get your readers on board.

Using online or agency translators

Maybe you don't use English as your everyday business language, but need it for a wider market. Then you'll naturally need to work out the best way to translate the language you do use into the right English for your objectives. As we've seen, you need to know whether this is standard, global or glocal English – perhaps varying with context.

To maintain professional credibility you need to verify your communication. This applies both if you do a translation in-house – perhaps with the aid of online translation tools or via multilingual staff – and if you outsource your translations to agencies. In either case, you're responsible for what ultimately goes out.

Even with agencies, there are consummate professionals who provide a first-rate service – but there are also agencies that get things wrong. Do some diligent research as it's your reputation, not just theirs, that's at stake when errors are made, or misunderstandings arise.

Now let's look at online translators. On occasion they hit the mark but sometimes they're completely wrong: seriously bad news for business. Don't be tricked into a false sense of security by thinking that all online translations make sense.

We wanted to understand a tweet in French that read:

> *Détecter les sujets émergents n'est pas qu'une affaire de mots clés.*

So we used Google to search for three free online-translator tools to get a translation into English. Here are the first two translations we sourced:

> *Detecter emergents subjects is not that an affair of words cles.*
> *Detecter the subjects emergents is not that a matter of words cles.*

And we have to say, these don't make any sense to a native English speaker. The third translation we found made a great deal more sense:

> *Detect emerging issues is not just about keywords.*

However, the translation tool was still unable to yield the correct form of the French verb '*détecter*' which should have been translated into English as 'to detect'.

Note also that the business world is increasingly using apps, for multi-functional smartphones. It's not for us to name in this book the tools that work or don't work, but to draw your attention to the potential problem. It's a rapidly evolving area.

So can you see how these translators may be 'free' on one level but if inaccurate they can ultimately cost you by undermining your credibility? Readers are likely to look at such writing and:

- They may indeed see it as rubbish.
- They are likely to move on or complain (to you and/or others).
- It will sabotage your communication objectives.

Can you ever justify using online translations? Yes, if you use them with care. Try to use the simplest expressions – and check they are really used in business today. Ask an English-speaking colleague or customer. Read current business books, online articles, etc, and look at major companies' websites in English. Get a feel for what works.

'Brand you' and your organization's brand

For the purpose of this book, 'brand you' is about establishing your personal mark through your business communication. How do you want to be seen? What do you want to be remembered for? We're not just talking about your non-verbal or spoken communication, it's also about your letters, your reports and also, very importantly today, through your e-mails (more on this in Chapter 6).

Every time you write at work, it's an opportunity to shine and create a good impression both within the business and beyond, in your wider readership. Get it right and you'll show yourself to be *clear, confident, smart* and *sophisticated* (as defined in Chapter 1). This will serve you well as your career progresses. Get it wrong, even if only briefly, and your personal credibility and value will be harmed, perhaps for a long time. In this digital age, your reputation can go viral, as never before.

It's a fact that everyone in a company has their own identity. What's not universal is how freely individuals are allowed to express this in their place of work. Effusive, extrovert cultures can welcome the individual openly making his or her mark. More reserved cultures and/or where the consensus of the group is the prime driver (before decisions can be taken) will naturally look at this differently. They believe in sticking together and working on better brand value of the professional organization they work in.

If we just look at India for another example, certain major Indian companies have actively decided to form company identities without incorporating religious values and customs. In contrast, many SMEs have even named their ventures after religious deities, such is their cultural setting. It's quite commonplace in the subcontinent.

So, all across the world, individuals have to co-exist with and, to varying degrees, depend on the identity of their business for which they work. Ideally all organizations anywhere in the world should make everybody feel valued. If personal self-development is encouraged, so should the fact that each person is an ambassador for that company.

If everyone embraces this concept, it's clear that every piece of writing you put out can actively market both 'brand you' (according to the constraints we've mentioned) and your organization's brand. Perhaps this is why we're seeing more and more professionals becoming entrepreneurs and running their own businesses, because it gives them the freedom to establish their own, unique brand and make a mark in their own ways, be it locally or globally.

We certainly suggest effective writing is a way you can be *seen to be* valuable to your valued reader and an asset to your company. Where others in your organization may get poor responses if their writing seems boring, in stark contrast you can give your audience the feel-good factor through your enthusiasm about what you do. They can feel 'warm' rather than 'cold' towards your suggestions, from the start. You might start to see replies such as 'Excellent. Great job done, thanks.' Alongside developing your personal brand, you'll be developing your career too.

Did you know that if you write down your aspirations you are more likely to achieve them? And what if we said the correct written English could double your chances of getting your dream job? Then we would be wrong. It could actually quadruple your chances: that's how important words are – and how important English is globally.

Activity

Why not jot down your work-related aspirations now? Let writing help make them happen!

_____

_____

_____

_____

_____

_____

Now let's bring word power to help you define 'brand you'. Think of a well-known brand. If we look at Coca-Cola (an example that probably everyone in business will have heard of), why is it well known? Largely because over years and years of clever global marketing, the company has made us able to identify the product and make it spring readily into our minds.

Have you ever been part of a branding exercise at work? It may not have been an explicit marketing assignment, but you might have played some part in creating a new project or launching a new product to end users.

People tend to get passionate about branding and give it their all. It can be when people give their best performance. But why should it be any different when you are thinking of starting a new job, career or venture? When the brand is you, look for your personal best.

Once you've created your brand, this can make you **confident** to excel at everything you do. To help you, which words in accessible global English accurately capture 'brand you'? Be honest. Whatever your culture, it's really best not to exaggerate. You have to deliver what you say you can, and, as always, be mindful that some cultures will value some qualities over others.

Maybe some of the following words and phrases fit the bill:

- highly motivated;
- enthusiastic;
- energized;
- hard-working;
- good communicator;
- self-driven;
- self-starter;
- team player.

It can help to ask colleagues what words they would use to describe you. Maybe they may come up with other suggestions, such as:

- high achiever (or over-achiever);
- trustworthy;
- conscientious;

- reliable;
- polite;
- considerate;
- good mediator;
- calm under stress;
- quality conscious;
- totally professional;
- paying attention to detail.

Activity

Can you think of any other qualities or other factors? List them here.

_____

_____

_____

_____

_____

_____

Understanding the image you should promote (at all times) is one way you can make your mark through business writing. You may be a Nobel-winning physicist, but if you just have to send one e-mail to a person that may be all that person knows about you.

Help readers to 'get to know you' through your writing. If you write blandly: 'It appears this may have some potential' your readers will most likely perceive you to be bland – and even worse, uninteresting and uninterested. On the other hand, if you express interest and enthusiasm, for example: 'I'm excited at this opportunity', you're far more likely to engage readers' attention and make your mark.

Grasp this potential for dual marketing (yourself and your organization) and you can transform your performance. You too can sell, even if you are not expressly part of your company's sales team. Naturally, we mean implicit selling (selling a message) as opposed to explicit selling (direct selling of goods or services for people to buy). It still counts because effective writing 'sells' personal expertise. And if we talk about a consistently professional, quality-conscious workforce, it has to mean everyone, every time, doesn't it?

Let's look at examples of written e-mails that may sell the writers short. These writers may feel they are totally professional – but their writing suggests otherwise. They may also be quite unaware of the judgement others may make based on this evidence.

Request for information

This e-mail was sent to an external provider by a company's training manager.

> **FROM:** celine@anymail.com
> **TO:** petersmith01@maillink.co.uk
> **SUBJECT:** Information request
>
> Hi. Cd u send a quotation for an induction course in biz management?
> Regards,
> Celine.

Recipient's likely perception:

'I think this should be presented more professionally. The opening greeting and abbreviations are overly informal, especially for the first point of contact. Why hasn't the writer introduced herself and her company? What are her precise needs? How can I send a quotation without any details at all? Where is the "please" or "thank you"? Does it really take much longer to write "Please could you..." or "business management"? This is not a private text: it's a corporate e-mail.

This writer has done nothing to promote either personal or company brand, has missed a golden opportunity and has instead sent an incomplete message that I will have to follow up for clarification before I can deal with it!

This writer's overly informal writing harms both her company's and her personal brand.'

Interim reply

This update was sent by e-mail to an internal colleague.

FROM: donna@gomail.com
TO: melanieg002@maillink.com
SUBJECT: Interim reply

Sorry this is late but I hope you don't mind. Please bare with us while we gather the remaining info.
Regards,
Donna.

Recipient's likely perception:

'There's some empathy here, which is good: at least this writer is sorry that the update is late. But actually, yes, I do mind that the update's late and I don't think she really cares.

Also, she could not be bothered a) to check the right spelling: "bear" not "bare", or b) write "information" not "info".

This writing is simply unprofessional and the writer has neither promoted her personal nor company brand well.'

Sending a presentation

This e-mail was sent to an external client.

FROM: andy@swiftmail.com
TO: tomjones003@maillink.com
SUBJECT: Presentation attached

Please find my presentation attached. I have to tell you at the outset that I haven't had much time to prepare, so there are sure to be mistakes.
Regards,
Andy

Recipient's likely perception:

'I really don't want to see a mistake-riddled piece of work. Don't I deserve first-class attention? I would have been much happier if Andy had taken more time to prepare and check the quality, even if it meant negotiating a slight extension of time.

I think both the company brand and the impression of the individual ('brand you') are damaged by this example of writing.'

Now let's look at some examples of how to promote brand you. They show how some business writers manage to put their imprint on everything they write. Even though a barrage of e-mail, their messages make us want to read them. Here are some e-mail extracts showing what we mean:

Dear <name>

Spring days, full of summer promise

I hope this e-mail finds you very well indeed.
The winter is over, the spring buds are awakening, so let me now introduce our summer schedule which is full of good things to look forward to.

E-mail disclaimer (part extract)
We have an environmentally-friendly e-mail policy and hope you share this with us. When we print an e-mail, we make sure we use recycled paper and we dispose of it responsibly. Please pass the message!

Diwali Offer: 20% Discount @ Mocha's

Dear Customer,
Diwali celebrations just got better with these coupons at Mocha's!
Please present this coupon at your branch of Mocha's to get a whopping 20% discount on any beverage.
Hurry, these coupons last till Oct 31!

Ultimately, 'brand you' is what you make it. Nobody can fill in the detail but you. We can't tell you how to define your personal brand – but we can encourage you to take time to think through the image you wish to present. Link this to the message you also need to project and do this consistently in your memos, e-mails, reports, letters, presentations, websites and brochures – in fact in everything you write in English.

Worksheet

Section A: Knowing your theory

Based on what you have understood from this chapter, respond to the following questions and statements by ticking the 'Yes' or 'No' boxes.

		Yes	No
1	By the term 'digital economy', we refer to the people, communications infrastructures and ever-developing technology that come together to provide a global platform for trade, social and other interactions.	☐	☐
2	Is it good to write on auto-pilot?	☐	☐
3	You should have an idea of what you need to achieve when you write to a colleague, customer or supplier.	☐	☐
4	Complicated words are always more impressive than simple words in business today.	☐	☐
5	Is there a cost involved if you have to correct written mistakes, for example in your company's brochures or on its website?	☐	☐
6	Should you use an English idiom if you don't fully understand it?	☐	☐
7	Reserved and extrovert cultures equally encourage staff to show individuality in their business writing.	☐	☐
8	Developing 'brand you' is something that only you can do.	☐	☐

Section B: Detailing your e-mails

Towards the end of this chapter, we see examples of where e-mails go wrong and give out unintended messages. Have you ever received such an e-mail? Indeed, have you ever sent an e-mail where your message was misunderstood? Why was that?

Below is an e-mail which is about to be sent to a customer, Mr Gordon Bennett. Can you spot any errors or gaps in communication here?

FROM: joebloggs@youwantitwehaveit.com
TO: gordanbennett@mailink.net
SUBJECT: Notification of package dispatch

Dear Mr Benet,

We are instructed that Order (reference number: ....) has been dispatched today. It is anticipated that it will arrive at your doorstep within the next seven working days.

Should you have any queries or complaints, you can contact us via e-mail helpdesk@youwantitwehaveit.com or call us on 0855 123 456.

We will endeavour to assist with your problem with immediate attention and effect and await your further instructions in the event you would like to order from us again.

Yours faithfully,

The Dispatch Team,

You Want It We Have It Pvt Ltd.

How would you rewrite this e-mail? Can you remove the errors? What about the tone – in the light of what you've read in this chapter, could you improve it? We have refreshed the subject heading, to help start you off, but there is still an error. Can you see it?

FROM: joebloggs@youwantitwehaveit.com
TO: gordanbennett@mailink.net
SUBJECT: Your package has been dispatched today!

Dear Mr...

Chapter Four
Common challenges in business English in a global workplace

Don't just focus on seeing things from your own perspective. It can give you blind spots.

Presentation, style and fonts matter

It's often said that when we meet someone face to face it can take about seven seconds to make that important initial impression. It can actually take fewer seconds to make a gut judgement about someone's writing.

We may not like it – and we may not even be aware of it – but the way we present our writing plays a huge part in how people perceive our competence. For example, if our writing is messy and unstructured, we cannot stop readers making a snap decision and value judgement that it's 'not good enough'. And it's an 'own goal', a problem of our own making if, as a result, readers think we are muddled and unprofessional.

We're sure you will have made some, if not all, of these judgements about other people's writing, at some point or other:

1 I like the look and feel of this.

2 This is important.

3 It's clearly in my interests to read this and react to it.

4 This is sincere: I like a company to care about my needs and serve me well.

5 This is enthusiastic and reasoned: I can 'buy into this'.

6 This seems like an organized business that knows what it is writing about.

7 I can make an informed decision based on this information.

8 I know what to do and when and it's easy.

9 What does this mean?

10 I cannot begin to think how to reply to this, so I'll put it to the bottom of my in-tray.

11 This is not important.

12 This is insincere and grovelling.

13 This is badly presented and looks boring.

14 This is disjointed. It probably represents the way the company does business.

15 There's too much hassle involved to know what to do or whether it's right for me.

16 Do I have to do anything or not? I'm busy, so I'll do nothing.

Activity

In the list above, have we left anything out in your opinion? If so, why not continue by listing examples of your own here.

_____

_____

_____

_____

_____

_____

If we now substitute the word 'customers' for 'readers', does this inspire you even more to get each message right first time? We certainly hope so. So do try to get positive responses such as those shown in numbers 1–8 by designing writing to achieve them. If you can't be bothered, then be prepared for the responses summarized in numbers 9–16!

Reading challenges

Eyes get tired from reading large amounts of text, especially on computer, tablet device or smartphone screens. That's why good web-writers break copy into sections. Often:

- they go on to subdivide these further with headings in bold;
- they introduce subheadings, links and bullet points;
- just by clicking on these links, readers can access further information, as and when they need it. The choice and the timing is theirs.

This makes for sound business practice. We also believe this trend should be adopted in report and other writing too, as you'll see later in the book.

Reading can present other visual challenges too. If you have dyslexia or the visual condition known as Irlen's syndrome, this can alter the way you see the written word. It can be tricky to keep a track of words on a line, so you may skip words. All the more reason for writers to understand they must design writing that *presents well*.

Make it your mission to keep up to date with developments. For example, did you know that there is a new typeface called *dyslexie*, specifically designed to help those with dyslexia?

Every manager in a business that uses global English should, ideally, be aware that dyslexics have difficulties distinguishing between some of the 26 letters in the Latin-based alphabet used in English. It could be that someone in their team suffers from the condition and needs support.

Colour coding information can sometimes be a great help for some readers, though you will need to do some research on what your readers like. In a global context, colours can definitely imply different things for different nationalities. There are even such things as 'lucky' or 'unlucky' colours depending on culture.

Red can signify 'stop' (an allusion to traffic lights) for some countries – or, by inference, 'that's wrong' (hence the 'red pen' approach many nationalities adopt when they correct the written mistakes of others).

Yet red represents good luck in Asia. Black, as another example, represents funerals in Europe though the colour white does that in India. For some, green can be the colour of jealousy, for others green is, for obvious reasons, now linked to 'eco-friendly'. Dark blue signifies learning for some. A useful tip is that if you are pitching to a particular country, using colours from their flag in your promotional material may be a very useful way of presenting colours that will work for them.

It's also useful to know that colour blindness affects quite a number of people, maybe more than you might imagine. Do you suffer from it, or do you know someone who does? We have come across a surprisingly high number in workshops we run. Some estimates are that colour blindness could occur to some extent in around 8 per cent of males of European origin (though only around half a per cent of females). The colours that cause most problems are red and green. It's a good idea to avoid red and green typeface on green or red paper because a colour-blind reader may not be able to distinguish between text and background. The same will apply if you use red and green together on your website, or on analytical diagrams.

Certain coloured paper can help print stand out for certain readers. For example, plain cream and pale yellow work well for many readers. On the other hand, a patterned background can make reading far more difficult for some. Unfortunately, we find a lot of patterned backgrounds in many promotional materials, including presentation slides.

Activity

Do any colours have a significant meaning for you? Have you researched whether any might be significant for your target audience? Are any of these relevant in a business context? If so, list them here.

_____

_____

_____

_____

_____

_____

Sometimes it's useful to use visuals and techniques such as pie charts, bar charts, pictograms and numbers (which many readers will find particularly useful) alongside your words.

Throughout this book we suggest it's a good idea to consider a corporate communication policy in order to communicate a consistent, professional image. It's much easier to reinforce an organization's values, or a brand, when documents have a common look and feel.

Don't, however, leave the choice entirely to your graphic designers. Important as their input is, you still need to liaise carefully with them. We've come across cases where multinational organizations have regretted not doing this. Why? It's because design agencies sometimes use fonts in clients' brochures that their clients can't reproduce at work. It's a shame, as this rather undermines the concept of a seamless corporate identity.

So what fonts should you choose? There are so many fonts available, variously described as serif or sans serif, depending on the number of strokes on the letters (sans serif have fewer). Readability is the prime consideration both for the home and global market, as some readers will find it physically difficult to read some fonts.

The UK Learning and Skills Council recommend Arial, Times New Roman and Helvetica, as they are generally considered comfortable to read. Other fonts such as Tahoma and Verdana are favoured by website designers for their readability online. Do keep abreast of developments though, because even fonts 'move on' and some are now definitely seen as 'old school'.

In normal circumstances, it's generally recommended that 10–12 point size is used for ordinary type and 14 point or larger for headings. This can be varied according to your target audience and may have to be increased for some readers. We once saw 7-point text used for a caption underneath a photograph relating to a pensioners' event. How exceptionally unhelpful that seemed for that particular readership.

If you write for a website, or have to write leaflets, for example, check what legislation may be in place in order to avoid disability discrimination.

In a business context, it's also important to ask yourself: do you want a font that readers see as artistic and creative? Or might solid and dependable be better? It may seem strange to write this way about fonts, but readers do have such perceptions. For example:

- Comic Sans MS can seem to indicate conversation and can be perceived as friendly, though some readers really don't like it.

- Times New Roman is readable but can seem old-fashioned these days.

- Verdana was designed as a font for writing online material.

- Century Gothic is viewed as artistic though many complain it's not easy to read.

- Arial and Tahoma are both chosen by many government offices and learning providers as being easy to read.

The look and feel of documents is also very important in any book about effective writing. How might your readers or customers feel about reading something that is over-embellished, especially if there's a really important message embedded in it? What might happen if you or your colleagues cannot be bothered to set out letters and other documentation the way your readers expect?

Activity

Jot down your views on the font used in the box above, which is called Gigi. Even before you tried to read the message, how did this piece of writing look to you?

_____

_____

_____

_____

_____

_____

For marketing purposes, Gigi is described as a 'joyful' font. Did you describe it that way? Have you come across it in business? We have, and we were surprised it was used. We have also received requests for information in the font in the box below – Script MT Bold.

> *Dear Sir,*
>
> *May we kindly request you to send us details of your courses in business writing.*
>
> *Your prompt reply will be highly appreciated.*
>
> *Yours faithfully*
>
> *(Name)*
>
> *Buyer*

Many native English readers will find this handwriting style easy enough to read. We have found it (and similar fonts) in use in Asian and Middle Eastern business writing in English. Some readers will definitely find it pleasing to the eye, adding the 'personal touch' that's right for their culture and contributing the right splash of local colour.

But in a global context, other readers might see it as rather flowery and not modern enough. Added to this, the typeface might be extremely difficult for some readers not fully used to the Latin-based English alphabet, or people who find it difficult to process things visually.

Perhaps you cannot decipher the Gigi text in the box above. As a direct contrast, you'll see below how much easier it is to read the text in Tahoma.

> The look and feel of documents is also very important in any book about effective writing. How might your readers or customers feel about reading something that is over-embellished, especially if there's a really important message embedded in it? What might happen if you or your colleagues cannot be bothered to set out letters and other documentation the way your readers expect?

The feedback we get in general is that 'spidery' fonts can be almost unintelligible – and, by inference, un-businesslike. The commercial outcomes can be as follows:

- Although there are times when a jokey font or slogan validly engages readers' attention, (as long as it's right for the culture), it's never good news for readers to view your core business as a joke.

- They may misunderstand your message.

- They may take the wrong action, or no action.

- They might come back to you for clarification (which costs you and them time and money).

- They might tell others about you (in a negative way).

So make an informed choice as to which font is right for your business and your readers. However, do be aware that much of the design and thought you put in may be lost when your work is sent to an electronic device. It's upsetting but it happens.

Underlining, italics and justifying margins

We see much less underlining in business writing today – largely because so much writing is electronic and we expect underlining to signify a hyperlink. We expect to be able to click on it – and be taken immediately to some new information. We're puzzled if it doesn't work.

There's also a distinct move away from using italics in business writing. You will find them in this book, for some examples or emphasis. Generally we try to avoid italics, as a block of text presented in this way can be difficult to read.

Sometimes you'll see writers mixing italics, capitals and even fonts. Even in a native English-speaking market this can make a document look rather haphazard, cluttered, messy and potentially bewildering for the reader.

Take a look at an extract from a leaflet advertising insurance.

If you think you *don't need insuring* against ACCIDENTS in the home
then it is <u>VITAL</u> that you
Read the Other Side of this Leaflet

Jot down your thoughts here on the way this is set out.

_____

_____

_____

_____

_____

_____

We wonder what you thought. On one level, we can see why the writer thought this might work. It's true our eyes do focus on the different messages because of the mix and match of styles. But although it may make impact, does it impress? One set of buyers might be put off buying from a provider who seems muddled and old-fashioned. Another set might be attracted to an insurer who seems to be well established, with some years of trading, just judging by the traditional typeface and layout.

None of us can please all our business readers all the time. But today's global writing does tend to be streamlined and punchy – that is, to the point. That's no doubt why a lot of readers would tell us this mailshot extract seems outdated, although it does make sense. Ultimately though, it's the sales results that will tell us if this writer's approach worked or not here. Results are what matter in business writing.

Before we leave the physical appearance of writing in English, we would like to mention a normal convention in business, which is to align margins on the left (called 'left justified') with ragged edges on the right of the page. Publishers often use margins on the right ('right justified') or equal margins on both sides ('justified').

Readability also depends on contrast between font, text block, headings and surrounding white (or other coloured) space. Spread text out and, as already mentioned, use size and colour to attract attention in the desired way. In short, design is an integral part of writing global business English.

The pitfalls of 'instant'

Because of information overload and 'fast load', we don't always take enough time *to think* about things. The problem is, even in our own language, that's how mistakes happen. So if you are a non-native English speaker writing business English, do factor in extra, not less, time than when you write in your own language. When it comes to writing, speed can accelerate problems, not solutions. For example, have you heard that some companies set up a two-minute delay before sending e-mails? It's not without reason, as we'll be discussing in Chapter 6.

Scan reading and skim reading

Today's online readers tend to scan read or skim read. They look at written text quickly to identify relevant information and to get an overview of contents. It is partly to do with processing information overload and it's partly because people want to reduce the number of words they have to read. It's also having an impact on the way we need to write paper reports, as we'll be covering in Chapter 9.

Here are some tips to help:

- Scan reading and skim reading are further evidence that readers are likely to react fairly instantly to the look of writing, so try to get it right for their needs first time.

- They are also likely to consider: will this writing help me now, or do I bookmark it for later? This is all the more reason to make initial impact – and maybe deliver fuller meaning later in the writing.

- You can help your written words make initial impact by choosing simple yet powerful words, great visuals, meaningful topic headings and subheadings and also by reinforcing messages.

- Non-native English readers, who may be overwhelmed by language they do not fully understand, can then have the opportunity to focus at the later (revisiting) stage on any words that they may need to look up.

Presentations should always showcase your talent

This section is about helping you realize the importance of the written word used in presentations or proposals, for example in your slides, handouts at the event or in a written follow-up, such as a casual e-mail afterwards.

Do you find giving a presentation fun? Few people do. Business presentations today are often very serious matters. In many ways they are 'the new report' for many organizations. This is particularly true in a global context, as slides can so easily be shared across the world.

So, they should have a clear business purpose. The same goes for your written proposal answering a request for information (RFI). In fact, a good written proposal can be the key to that first and crucial step inside a potential customer's door.

Any proposal you write may be passed around and judged when you are not there to explain it. The same applies to the written slides behind your spoken presentation. Yet presenters often overlook this, for some strange reason. Why is this, when written word power takes centre stage here too? The reality can be that when you fluff (make a mistake with) a spoken word, your audience may be too busy fixing their attention on that typographical error in your slide to notice!

If we try to capture the experience of a presentation in words, we could start with 'lights, camera, action' – in our minds at least. Because staff in a company to whom you are pitching for new business may give you the stage for say, a maximum of 15 minutes. This is the time when you need to be a **smart** and **sophisticated** performer to be **successful**.

This will be an immense help when you may have as little as 10 minutes to pitch – and just 5 minutes to answer questions. So as not to waste your time or your audience's time, create a spotlight that shines on you. Showcase your talent. But don't put your audience in the shade: they are extremely important too.

If you don't go flat out to ensure that the presentation or talk propels you into your target company's future, why bother to be there?

Remember, most presenters run out of time. That's why great written slides and handouts with the right call to action become invaluable. They can sell for you, after you have left. Another point to remember is that you can create a position of strength by being a non-native English presenter.

Whatever you do, don't get noticed for the wrong reasons. You will be noticed one hundred times more for using a wrong or obscure word than for avoiding it and choosing the correct or simpler word that everyone understands.

We are sorry to say a real-life presentation slide we have seen contained bullet points with these errors:

- We need to develop this customer expereince.
- We need to decide if there servces are needed.

Have you spotted the mistakes?

The bullet points should have read:

- We need to develop this customer experience.
- We need to decide if their services are needed.

Have you seen any errors in people's presentation slides recently? Did you react in any way? If so, how? You might like to jot down here anything you have noticed in the past, or from now on. A good exercise would be to ask colleagues to swap notes with you. That way you'll get a feel for what distracts people from the messages that the presenter intended.

_____

_____

_____

_____

_____

_____

Be seen in the right light, whether it's an internal or external presentation that you're delivering. In terms of quality, why differentiate? A presentation should always be good. Your internal presentation may be for the people who hold the purse strings or are key influencers. If you are **confident**, you will never settle for second best again!

So, how do you make your presentation to optimum effect? What are the particular challenges you will face when presenting in English? Is there any way you can actually use these to your benefit? You might find it helpful to approach these questions from different angles.

Activity

Ask yourself the following, as relevant:

- Do I want to remind readers in a positive (not apologetic) way that I'm not a native English speaker?
- Can I actively get them on my side by asking them to stop me at any time to explain anything that they need to understand better?
- Do I want to impress them with perfectly composed slides?
- Would it help to talk them through a 'road map' at the outset?

In this context, to provide a 'road map' means creating and explaining a structure to your presentation and sticking to it. It means, particularly in an audience of mixed cultures and differing levels of business English competency, you're less likely to see a sea of blank faces in front of you. That's because people can navigate the path with you. They won't get lost, even if momentarily diverted for any reason (for example, if a latecomer interrupts them). It manages expectations: always a good idea in global communication.

Don't undermine being **confident** in your ability from the start, for example by apologizing before you've uttered a single word of your presentation. We've heard people say: '*I'm sorry if this seems unprepared: I didn't have much advance notice*' and '*Please forgive me in advance; I'm quite nervous about presenting.*'

Isn't this an unnecessary sign of weakness? It's almost saying: 'This is not going to be good. I know it and you'll know it soon enough.' Already you will have members of your audience wondering why they bothered to come. So, instead, create a position of strength. Face the people in your audience confidently and invite them to stop you at any stage if they need you to explain the words you use. By doing this:

- They sense your confidence.
- They sense that you know what you are talking about.
- They appreciate your care about helping them follow where you lead.

Anticipate what may be asked

Every presentation should enable a dialogue. People in the audience may ask questions you haven't covered, question you on something that wasn't clear, or on a slide that contained an error. If you have really anticipated their likely questions and presented tightly and well, you'll find any questioning is reduced – and has the right focus on your primary objectives. You won't lose time – and face – by having to answer questions with what could be seen as a weak reply, such as: 'I knew you'd ask that!' Members of a harsh audience from an expressive culture might say: 'Well, if you knew we would ask that, then why didn't you cover it?'

Those in an audience from a reserved culture might not show their displeasure at your lack of professionalism in not getting it right. That doesn't mean they won't feel it. They might even be offended by any omission on your part. Their unspoken feelings might be that if you knew something hadn't been covered, then why are you wasting their time not giving the answers they need?

More tips to make business communications easier

Create an opportunity for follow-up dialogue

If you don't already have attendees' e-mail addresses, it's a good idea to ask for them if they would like you to e-mail a summary to them, after the event. This will be useful for them, especially if you have included helpful tips in the summary. It's useful for you too, as it takes you into a future with those people. Your short talk may be over but you have scheduled yourself more time with those delegates. You are not cold-calling them: they have asked for more. This means it becomes a two-way process: an excellent outcome.

Eliminate the guesswork – rely on yourself

Microsoft PowerPoint still dominates in presentations today. Just the fact that it is electronic can lead to potential problems, including unfamiliar operating systems, hyperlinks that don't work, even power failures. A good written preparation (at least for yourself) makes sure you can carry on. So don't just rely on technology: rely on yourself!

Activity

What is your back-up plan in case your PowerPoint slide show doesn't work? Describe it here.

_____

_____

_____

_____

_____

Going back to your presentation, don't use words you are unsure of. Check that members of your audience understand from time to time, especially on words of a technical nature. This is particularly important in multicultural groups where a commonly known English word may sound quite different when spoken with a foreign accent or transliterated on a slide.

We've already highlighted how people from some cultures and also with some personalities can be reluctant to speak up to ask, for fear of embarrassment. What experience shows us is that, time after time, people who don't really understand a particular word or phrase try their hardest to work out the meaning based on something similar from their own language. And very often this is entirely wrong, unfortunately for all. What is our tip? Don't be afraid to ask and clarify. It is a strength not a weakness, and everybody benefits by speaking a common language that really is common currency.

Worksheet

Section A: Knowing your theory

Based on what you have understood from this chapter, respond to the following questions and statements by ticking the 'Yes' or 'No' boxes.

		Yes	No
1	It takes only a few seconds to form an impression when reading a business document.	☐	☐
2	Is being aware of disabilities such as dyslexia and colour-blindness important when it comes to designing websites and brochures?	☐	☐
3	A jokey font always works wonders for attracting customers to your business.	☐	☐
4	Readability also depends on contrast between font, text block, headings and surrounding white (or other coloured) space.	☐	☐
5	Both writing too quickly and skim reading can create problems.	☐	☐
6	Are presentations purely about the spoken word?	☐	☐
7	Is it a good idea to have a 'road map' at the start of a presentation so that your audience understands the presentation's structure and sequencing?	☐	☐
8	When it comes to delivering presentations, is it necessary to anticipate any questions your audience may ask?	☐	☐

Section B: Presenting in a global context

This chapter has looked at the various factors involved in the look and feel of business and marketing documentation, for example presentations, websites and brochures. These factors are important to consider as they affect the readability of the documents which could lead to misunderstandings and miscommunications because of faulty presentation. So, what is your view on presentation? You perhaps already have an idea, but to have a clearer picture, try the following exercises:

- Choose some marketing documentation from any business organization you like (this can be the one you work for, or your own, or one you pick at random) and take a good look at how the organization has presented it.

- How clear is its brand image? How easy or difficult is it to read the content? What colours has it used and how has it used them? Make notes as you study these points, to help you remember your observations.

- Now think about how you would redesign the marketing documentation you have chosen, to make it look and feel better. What would you change? (Consider fonts, text colours, line spacing, paragraph alignment, background colours, etc).

- Make your changes and see what the fruits of your imagination have led you to create.

Chapter Five
How does writing in a global economy affect us all?

"Words are actually for communication. You wouldn't always guess that, the way some companies write to their customers...

In a sense we are all selling now

In Chapter 3 we highlighted how this is the time of the digital economy – when people, communications infrastructures and ever-developing technology come together to provide a global platform for business, trade, social and other interactions. In effect this has made us all writers now and, in a sense, we are all sellers too. Even if we're not actively selling our wares, instinctively we should be marketing our organization and selling its messages every time we write. We always need to reach those in our audience, not 'draw the blinds and close the door' to exclude them. That's what ineffective communication will do.

You sell your messages when your readers see them and say:

- 'Yes, this is in our interests.'
- 'We know what we must do, why, how and when.'
- 'We feel appreciated.'
- 'This is definitely the product, service or message of our choice.'

If you achieve these reactions, you are indeed an effective ambassador and salesperson for your organization, whatever your actual job specification.

Effective writing opens doors

Have you noticed an overall decrease recently in 'cold calling'? By this we mean the practice where companies make their first, unannounced point of contact with you, usually by telephone. Cold calling aside, you probably use the telephone far less at work today than even a few years ago. Texting and other electronic messaging now prevail because they are cheap and fast, which are their plus points. On the minus side though, you may be tricked into thinking electronic messages are altogether easier. In fact, to succeed you may have to work that little bit harder than you thought if you want to open the door to new business. Why? It's because when you are that voice on the telephone, you have an opportunity (however fleeting) to put over your messages with your own personal touch. You can ask and answer questions as soon as they arise, and try to develop rapport with the people you're working with.

Activity

What are the pros and cons of using the telephone versus writing in the course of your work? Which do you find easier and why?

Telephone		Writing	
Pros	Cons	Pros	Cons

Make writing an effective point of contact (POC)

Why not start by looking at things as if you are the consumer who is thinking of making a purchase? Imagine you're thinking of attending a training event on a particular topic. There are a number of providers you could use, so you send a request for information (RFI) by e-mail to two different companies with website offerings (subject and price) that seem to fit your requirements.

Here are extracts from the two replies you receive (also by e-mail).

Training provider A

I understand that u want to know more about the event and wats the procedure for u to join? It's all in the file attached ☺

Training provider B

Thank you very much for your request for information. We attach details of the training event that we feel will best suit your needs. Do let us know if this is what you are looking for, or would you like us to call you to see if we can customize a bespoke package?

Which written communication are you likely to favour? Feedback consistently suggests that most people will be drawn to professionalism. Training provider B is likely to have the edge. Writers can think brevity is a virtue – but it won't be if it's at the expense of customer relations. The text speak ('u' for 'you') that training provider A has used in the e-mail can also be seen as disrespectful in business and the mistake ('wats' for 'what's') is regrettable. Customers routinely make the judgement that an organization that cares about presentation is likely to put a value on quality and a systematic approach generally. Writing well is an opportunity to open a door to new customers. Don't waste it.

Talking about opening doors, CVs are meant to do just that. (CVs are called resumés in the United States, France and elsewhere and 'biodata' in the East.) Yet we constantly hear from recruiters that sloppy, mistake-riddled, unstructured and unfocused CVs are deleted or binned straightaway. Procurement managers also disregard shoddily presented bids and proposals. They frequently comment that if applicants can't be bothered to answer the brief, or get details right, why should they get the contract? There are always others who do take care and are accurate.

All cultures sense carelessness as disrespectful; people who deliver the bare minimum can be seen to be disrespectful of others and probably lacking in self-belief too. That's why we want to help people be **confident** and be seen as **smart** by always delivering the best business communication they can.

So do get into the habit of looking at your writing objectively. That way, you'll soon manage to identify the words, formats and presentation of material that make the right impact. Your writing will build bridges to enable readers 'to cross to your side' instead of 'pushing them away' as a lot of writing does, often unintentionally.

Letters: A general introduction

The way companies have to write for customers today varies greatly from the way they would have written years ago. It's noticeable that we write far fewer letters in business today than even in the recent past. E-mail communications are now largely taking their place, though letters are not extinct yet. Whether you send them traditionally by post (sometimes referred to nowadays as snail mail) or electronically, here are some tips to help.

1 **Identify the purpose of your letter and identify who your readers are.** Is the purpose of your letter to inform? If so, why? Is it to instigate action? If so, what action? Who by? How? When by? These questions relate to the purpose of your letter. In addition, do try to have some understanding about those in your audience. They are real people. You need to show you care about them – and also that you care how they feel about you and your organization.

2 **Identify the format.** Do you use templates? Do you use a subject heading above your main text? Do you use a reference

or code? An informative subject heading can engage your reader's attention from the start. It also helps you identify the point of your letter. Customize it if you can. Even the use of the word 'Your', as in 'Re: Your contract XYZ', is more reader-friendly than 'Re: Contract XYZ'. (Out of interest, you do not need to use 'Re:' at all – it is a question of house style and may be one of the points you identified in the worksheet exercise at the end of Chapter 2.)

3 **Identify how well your letters work.** Try to get in the habit of asking yourself questions such as these each time: Did I achieve the right result from this letter? Or was there a problem? If so, did I cause the problem or was it because of something else? If there was a problem, try to work out why that was. It may have been because you have not worded something clearly. It may be because the person had not paid sufficient attention to what you said. If you discover what you might need to do differently next time you write, you're highly likely to improve the results you need. The time you spend analysing these points becomes your investment in future success.

Activity

Have you ever had a response that demonstrated somebody had mis-understood your communication? Was it because of flaws (mistakes, missing information, and so on) in the correspondence you sent? If so, it can help you to list the flaws here, so that you avoid the same problem in the future. You may find it useful to swap notes with colleagues too. In particular, was your communication insufficiently **clear** and **comprehensible** – or were there other reasons?

_____

_____

_____

_____

_____

_____

Specific tips on salutations and titles – how to address people

Always check the spelling of the name of the person you are writing to and use his or her correct job title. We know that readers are quickly (and justifiably) offended when their personal details are incorrect. It can be difficult though, for example if you don't know whether the name you have been given relates to a male or female. Ideally, make enquiries: maybe someone else will know. Or you could use the person's full name at the beginning of the letter, for example: 'Dear Chris Palmer' – to avoid embarrassment or offence.

Titles used to address people

Some standard titles used to address people in English are:

- Mr (after which you write an adult male's name, whether the person is single or married);
- Master (after which you write a male child's name);
- Mrs (after which you write a married female's name);
- Ms (after which you write the name of an adult female who may, or may not, be married);
- Miss (after which you write the name of a female child or (young) unmarried female).

Years ago, it was the practice to write 'Mr.' and 'Mrs.' punctuated with a full stop (or period). This punctuation highlighted the fact that the words were abbreviations of the words 'mister' and 'mistress' respectively. Common practice today is to write both words with open punctuation 'Mr' and 'Mrs'.

Another title in common use is 'Dr'. It is the title used for both male and female medical doctors, as well as for postgraduates with a Doctor of Philosophy degree (PhD or DPhil). So, for example, you write: 'Dear Dr Smith' and there is no indicator as to whether Dr Smith is male or female. For some unknown reason, English does not make this distinction, but some languages do. For example, the German 'Herr Doktor' translates to 'Mr Doctor' in English, or 'Frau Doktor' translates to 'Mrs Doctor'.

Take care to spell names correctly. Get it wrong and the chances are you will find out the hard way: your recipients may complain to you, or about you. Naturally, there will also be further commercial implications if compliance-related documentation has wrong details. The repercussions can be serious and costly on many levels.

It would be difficult for us to set out all the salutation possibilities for addressing people globally, so we really encourage you to carry out further research relating to your target audience. You'll find it really strengthens cross-cultural understanding to ask professionals from different countries for tips on how to get it right. For example, a very helpful, courteous engineer from The United Arab Emirates (UAE) gave us tips on Arabic culture in business writing. He feels that, in general, Arabic culture is close to East Asian cultures when it comes to respect. Respectful letter writing is the norm and the beginning of a letter or e-mail would start with something similar to 'Kind greetings' or 'We extend our greetings and best wishes to you and your company' before going on to discuss the subject matter. Arabic business letters usually end with a salutation such as 'Please accept our admiration and appreciation' and would never end with terms of endearment between genders, such as 'with love' or 'yours' to avoid misinterpretation.

So it's not hard to see how an expressive Western culture could so unintentionally offend a formal, respectful culture with expressions such as 'thanks, honeybun, lol' – even though it is meant to be friendly and grateful. And then we have to remember that even in the West, as just one example, not all cultures are expressive in the same way. On German blogs we sometimes find posts that suggest that enquiring after personal matters is not appropriate in business. It can be seen as wasting time or being too inquisitive. Therefore we all have to listen, in order to learn what's best for our audience.

So how can you get it right? The answer has to be: take time to find out what your audience expects. Your writing will be more effective and **successful** as a result, and you'll understand how doing business globally literally broadens your horizons. This really is the **smart** and **sophisticated** approach to writing.

Before we leave this section, have you ever seen a letter addressed 'To whom it may concern' and wondered why this was used? Well, a writer uses it when he or she does not know who the recipient will be. For example, if you are a contractor leaving one assignment, the company you have worked for may give you an open reference such as this:

To Whom It May Concern

Fred Jones designed and successfully implemented a software programme company-wide for us from June–September this year. He delivered the programme on time and within budget and we found him to be a consummate professional at all times.

Gert Braun
Brunner BV

Example of a letter asking for information

This book is not designed to give you writing templates because when it comes to writing global English 'one size' won't 'fit all'. We explain throughout how you need to customize what you do according to those in your target audience and their locale.

What follows is, therefore, simply an outline example of how to write a letter in English. Even within the UK there are differing conventions as to where to place the date and address on a letter, and what salutations or endings to use, among other considerations. Other countries will naturally have differing conventions too. So once again, you need to adapt the outline according to your needs – and then think about whether it could be included in your company's style guide.

Here is an outline of how to set out a business letter in English.

Your company name and contact details
Addressee's name and job title
Addressee's organization's name
Number or name of building
Name of street or road

Post town
County or district
Postcode (UK English) or area code or zip code (US English)
Country

Date

Reference number

Opening salutation – with or without a comma, depending on house style

Heading

Main body of text

Closing salutation – with or without a comma, depending on house style

Name of writer
Position in organization

Enc. (Refers to enclosures, if there are any.)

Now let's look at the outline in practice. Below is a fairly standard letter from a company asking another for some further information regarding a proposed project.

Version 1

This is where the writer doesn't know the name of the person he or she is writing to:

The Managing Director
Trans-Continent Projects Ltd
21–24 Any Street
Anytown
AB3 4CD
UK

16 December 2012

Your reference: DT/01/1870

Dear Sir or Madam,
Your proposed waste-recycling projects

We understand that you are launching several waste-recycling projects over the next ten years and are looking for companies who can assist you.

As a company with leading expertise in this area, we would be very interested in making a bid to be a partner in the design and implementation of the projects we have seen on show at the Town Hall. For this reason, we would be grateful if you could forward us further details in this connection.

Yours faithfully,*

John Smith
Director
Smith Holdings

Enc. Please find our company brochure enclosed, as an introduction to our company.

*Note that this is the UK English convention when writing to someone whose name you do not know. In US English you will find such a letter could end with: 'Sincerely' or 'Best regards' or 'Yours truly'. In Indian English you will find letters end with 'Thanks and regards' or 'Yours faithfully' or 'Kind regards'.

Version 2

You can adapt the opening and closing of the preceding letter where you know the person's name. Then, for example, you can write: 'Dear Mr Smith (Mrs Smith, Ms Smith or Miss Smith)' (formal use of surname) or 'Dear Yusuf (or Sara)' (informal use of first name). When you end the letter, you write 'Yours sincerely' (followed by your name).

Do try to make sure you have the right name of the person to whom you are writing. Check whether the recipient's culture accepts you calling the person by his or her first name. Asian and Arab cultures, to name just two, can prefer the use of 'Ma'am' or 'Madam' and 'Sir' to the use of first names, unless you have been given a person's permission to do otherwise.

Be aware too that it can be difficult for differing cultures to identify what actually is a foreigner's first or family name. As relationship building can be crucial to business success, it is really respectful and worthwhile to get this right. Better to ask if you are not sure than to get it wrong.

Activity

How do business letters start and end in the work culture you follow? You could make a list here. If you need to alter these for your target audience, make a note of this too.

_____

_____

_____

_____

_____

_____

Should the same letter go to all recipients?

When writing business letters different approaches may be needed for different recipients. In business we often have to convey some difficult messages and when communicating globally, not only do we have to consider how **comprehensible** our communication is, we also have to show how we value people's custom, as well as culture.

Let's take as an example the type of letter that, unfortunately, you're likely to have to send out from time to time – chasing people for non-payment of accounts. Should you really send the same wording to really valued customers as to those who are known to be a possible risk? Naturally all customers matter, but every business also needs payment to survive. We suggest here how different approaches may help.

Writing to a valued customer

You have seen by now how culture and personality have an impact on tone. So if your natural tone may be in danger of sounding too harsh for some customers, here's one way you could soften it.

We do not appear to have received payment for invoice RD 78 for £780.57 which was due at the end of last month, in accordance with the agreed terms.

Please could you make payment within seven days, or let us know if there are any problems of which we are unaware?

If you have already paid this account, please ignore this letter and accept our apologies.

Writing to a customer who you feel is a bad risk

Here is an extract from a letter a company is writing to a customer who has ignored requests to pay an account.

You have not replied to our letters of 18 February or 22 April and we have been instructed by our accounts department to request immediate payment of this overdue account.

Payment should be made to this office at the above address within the next seven days, *or we may have no alternative but to take further action to recover this amount.*

Can you see how the style in the second example is much heavier-handed than in the first example? Don't use this heavy-handed style too readily, only when there is a real problem. If you know a final demand – rather than a request for payment – is the only course of action, then yes, you do need to stress that the customer must pay. Nevertheless, can you see how the passive construction '*we have been instructed by our accounts department*' helps the writer make the situation seem less personal? It's because any (implied) legal action against the customer will be by a department, not by the person who is writing. That can be useful so as not to jeopardize the relationship you may have worked hard to develop with that customer – which we know can be a very important cultural consideration. If we look at the writer's words '*or we may have no alternative but to take further action*' he or she manages to lessen the harshness once again, by using the verb 'may' rather than 'will'.

In this chapter, we have dealt with common challenges in business writing in a global workplace. We hope you can see how customers the world over are precious and our communication must show them that. To offend them should not be an option.

Worksheet

Section A: Knowing your theory

Based on what you have understood from this chapter, respond to the following questions and statements by ticking the 'Yes' or 'No' boxes.

	Yes	No
1 As long as you can reach out to the people in your target audience and get them interested in your product, service or business through your writing, then you are a potential salesperson, no matter what profession you are in.	☐	☐
2 Does knowing something about who your readers are help you communicate more effectively?	☐	☐
3 Is it important to know the form of salutation to use when you do business with an organization outside your own country?	☐	☐
4 Does it matter if you spell names of customers and colleagues wrongly?	☐	☐
5 When it comes to chasing customers who have not paid their accounts, should you send the same wording to really valued customers as to those who are known to be a possible risk?	☐	☐

		Yes	No
6	For international advertising to work, it's important for a business to strike a balance between local and global points of interest.	☐	☐
7	Standard written templates for letters work best globally.	☐	☐
8	By merely translating a marketing brochure from another language into English, are we sure to be communicating effectively?	☐	☐

Section B: Writing it right

This chapter looked into the many ways communication can be effective and ineffective, especially now that global businesses are trading through a digital economy.

Using the examples and looking at the letter templates in this chapter, try the following exercises.

Write a business letter to a potential customer, whose name you have acquired, telling them about your products or services and to ask the person if he or she would be interested.

Write a business letter chasing up a valued customer who has not paid a monthly account for the past two consecutive months.

Chapter Six
Writing e-mails

Think before you write, while you write – and definitely after you've written.

Evaluate when to use e-mail

Billions of e-mails are sent worldwide each day: a staggering figure that underlines the importance of the medium. They are the major business communication today, written by all levels of staff, in all types of company.

More often than not, staff deal with this written communication without formal training. It's strange really, as in the past companies routinely trained employees in paper letter or report writing, or offered secretarial support to maintain the right professional image.

The sheer volume we write or receive makes it essential to work out how best to use e-mail. The minute you've felt overly stressed before going on vacation (or after it) because of e-mail backlog in your inbox is the minute you realize e-mail can be the problem rather than the solution.

To reduce the stress of overload, companies should probably question more whether e-mail is the right communication medium for the business purpose in question. If, for example, people work in an open plan office, might it be better to talk to a person face to face? Alternatively, might telephone contact be the better medium sometimes? Occupational psychologists suggest this is often a better route to problem solving, and can make it easier to develop trust and relationships.

Interestingly, some companies are beginning to suggest e-mail could, in time, go the way of the fax (by being consigned to history) as this case study shows.

CASE STUDY Atos Origin

In February 2011 global IT and business technology company Atos Origin set out its ambition 'to be a zero e-mail company within three years'. As its global press release put it: 'Time to ease information pollution...'

CEO Thierry Breton announced that the volume of e-mails the company was at that time sending and receiving was unsustainable for business. Managers were spending between 5 and 20 hours per week reading and writing e-mails. Estimates were that only about 10 per cent of the 200 or so electronic messages staff received each day were actually useful and that it was time to think differently.

For this reason, Breton wanted his company's 49,000 staff to focus more on using instant messaging and chat-style collaborative services such as we see on Facebook or Twitter. The company believes that 'innovative social business solutions provide a more personal, more immediate and importantly, more cost effective means to manage and share information that supports the way of working in the 21st century and enables the Smart Organization.'

So, although the use of business e-mail may seem to be rising globally as we write, with initiatives such Atos Origin's, it may decline as social media grows in usage. In either event, business writing remains crucial. In e-mail, the focus is on the one-to-one recipient or the relatively 'captive audiences' of your e-mail thread or address book contacts. In social media, the focus is on writing to interest and thereby engage a wider, though specifically targeted, audience. We discuss this further in Chapter 12.

Activity

What is your general opinion about the quantity and nature of work e-mails? How many e-mails do you write and send on a typical working day? How many do you receive? Of those how many do you need to read? How many are actually useful and help your work performance? Note your findings here.

_____

_____

_____

_____

_____

_____

Were you surprised at your findings? Why not share them with colleagues?

So yes, you need to work out whether e-mail is the right communication medium for the message you need to send. Once you've established it is the right tool, in this chapter we suggest you also assess:

- Is e-mail used efficiently? (It will help to refer to your findings in the last activity.)
- Are all staff using e-mail in a professional, consistently corporate way?
- Should there be office guidelines on language and tone? (For example on level of formality or informality; and where to use local versus global English.)

Using e-mail efficiently

A good business e-mail achieves its business purpose and works as intended for you, your organization and your audience. A good e-mail is professional. It's addressed correctly, is sent to the right person, at the right time, in the right way – with the correct information and any necessary attachments, and the right people copied in, if need be. A good e-mail is also structured, so the recipient can see why he or she has received it and what action is required, if any.

Being systematic makes things seem easy. So let's look at the components in a bit more detail.

Understand the nature of the medium

Time and time again, readers the world over complain about poor tone and lack of manners in business writing today. Most of the complaints are about electronic writing, which naturally includes e-mail. Complaints largely arise because writers tend to see most electronic writing as chatting. That may be fine for personal e-mail but not for business e-mail.

Defining style for business e-mail is quite a tricky area. Even until fairly recently, the corporate consensus seems to have been that e-mail sits halfway between conversation and formal writing. That said, more recently we are finding legal contracts, insurance policies, travel documents and other official communications now routinely sent by e-mail – and they will always have to be classed as formal documentation. So the advice we give is don't let your professional guard down and don't let your e-mail or indeed any of your electronic writing be seen as inferior-quality writing.

This is a conundrum that applies across the board, as we see in Skype and social media generally. The consequence to avoid is for writers to think that a more 'social' medium is an excuse to become sloppy in their writing. Or to think that brevity means cutting out the right tone. Or not to think about what they want to communicate before they write. So, in effect, it takes longer to get the relevant information to perform a task, although the information reaches you faster. Add these factors together and you don't get a recipe for professionalism, do you?

Here are some real-life e-mail extracts that show great variation in style and tone:

- *Why haven't you done what I asked you yesterday?*
- *Thanks loads ☺.*
- *Therefore, although it is imperative that some assessment is made, it would appear that this is probably not the right channel in which to raise the matter at the current time but it might be advantageous to seek a more opportune moment in the not too distant future.*

Activity

What do you think of each example? Would any of the examples be right for your target audience? If not, can you think of better ways to write each one? Try it now. Straight after this exercise, we'll give your our views.

_____

_____

_____

_____

_____

_____

These are our comments on each example:

- *Why haven't you done what I asked you yesterday?* To some cultures this will appear overly direct and unfriendly. To others it will seem efficient and correct. What did you think?

  It was written by an Asia-Pacific employee who has only just started to write English at work. Previously he would have conducted much more business in face-to-face meetings, where he's known to be very friendly. In fact at the meeting that followed this e-mail he was all smiles. He would no doubt be disappointed to know some people would find him rude based on this one-line extract.

- *Thanks loads* ☺. To some cultures, a two-word reply with an emoticon will appear overly casual. To others it absolutely 'ticks the box'. What did you think?

  This is another good example of where writers need to gauge a target audience's expectations before sending this type of communication. It may work – but it really may not. Just by formalizing the message, the writer could better project 'brand you', the **sophisticated** professional image he or she wants.

  We suggest you look again at our advice on use of salutation in letters in Chapter 5, as the tips apply here as well. For example, check whether 'Hi' is the right way to address recipients, or whether a more formal greeting might be appropriate sometimes, or always.

  To give you the background, the writer of this e-mail extract was a UK employee who knew it was acceptable to use 'Hi' as a greeting in her workplace, as well as other informal language. She was also in the habit of sending these friendly emoticons internally. Some recipients found it acceptable, others did not. Those who did find it acceptable, subsequently 'read between the lines' if she did *not* send a happy face emoticon with her reply. It made them wonder if they had done something wrong.

Sometimes colleagues forwarded her e-mails to external readers, as part of an e-mail exchange. Very often these readers were unimpressed by the overly informal language. In fact, this is a common pitfall in any organization: e-mail threads are often sent, without review, to others who may not have been the intended recipients (for some of the thread at least). This can cause embarrassment. Has it ever happened to you or your colleagues?

- *Therefore, although it is imperative that some assessment is made, it would appear that this is probably not the right channel in which to raise the matter at the current time but it might be advantageous to seek a more opportune moment in the not too distant future.*

Some cultures may not have a problem with this extract but we actually think that, the world over, readers are likely to find it overly formal and old-fashioned. Did you?

Many of the words are not accessible global English and there's not a single 'people' word to inject vitality. We'll be giving you tips on how to do that in the next chapter. The sentence is strictly correct, in the sense of being free of mistakes, but could you instantly understand it on first reading? We doubt it. This extract is not easily **comprehensible** or **smart** for business today.

You are seeing throughout that writing tips don't have to change a great deal according to the medium. The same principles apply. Taking tone as an example, before you press 'Send' on your e-mail draft, check:

- Is this e-mail written professionally and correctly for purpose? (there is more on this in Chapter 8).
- Is my tone and vocabulary right for my local and/or global audience?
- Is my e-mail polite and does it convey a *virtual handshake*, to pull the readers towards me and my company – rather than push them away?

- Have I invited comments from my readers periodically, to check they understand and will respond the way I expect?
- Are there aspects of an e-mail chain which may irritate, embarrass or even cause offence, either in a local or cross-cultural context?

Structure matters

People generally understand that business writing should have some sort of structure. We could look on it as a jigsaw that needs its components to join together to make complete commercial sense.

So why do e-mails so often appear disorganized? It's generally because people tap the keys and write:

- words that just come out of the top of their heads, without structure;
- with no stated objectives;
- with no attention to spelling, punctuation and grammar and other quality controls;
- with no attention to layout;
- with no call to action or other required follow-up.

Here's an example of what we mean.

This e-mail was sent internally by a colleague to his HR Director, Hana Malik:

FROM: claessmit01@maillink.co.uk
TO: hanamalik01@maillink.co.uk
SUBJECT: Information Request

Hi Hana
In answer to yr enquiry, there are eight engineering trainees and 5 production trainees being trained at present (excluding the current final year trainees) and there are an additional six trainees who will start their training in November 2012. In total there are therefore 19 trainees who will be at various stages of their training from November 2012.
Hope this helps,
Claes

In his mind, the writer has fully answered Hana Malik's request for information. But is the information well presented? If not, why not? Put another way, if the director had asked for a report, would Claes have set out the information so haphazardly?

Activity

Could you improve the subject heading of Claes' e-mail? Could you improve the structure and style? There are many ways of approaching this activity: we just want you to see if you could structure the e-mail more clearly and helpfully.

FROM:
TO: hanamalik01@maillink.co.uk
SUBJECT:

Write the correct subject heading and refresh regularly, to help your readers. People might be surprised to know how irritated their colleagues or customers can be when they receive e-mails:

- without a subject heading;
- with a badly thought-through subject heading;
- with an out-of-date or non-refreshed subject heading.

You are sure to have come across the first issue and the chances are you open these e-mails last. It's human nature to open named documents first. If the e-mail is from an external source, you might even delete it, making the assumption that as there's no header it must be spam that has got through the filter.

If readers open an e-mail with a header in the second category, they can be less than impressed. The perception can be: 'If the writer doesn't seem to know what the e-mail is about, how can I or why should I?' Or they might simply be irritated at having to work it out for themselves. Isn't that the job of the professional who sent it? Harsh maybe, but feedback consistently suggests this.

The e-mail sent with the out-of-date or non-refreshed subject heading is probably the most frequent offender. It really can be business inefficiency at its height and is too often found in e-mail threads or chains, where people reply to one message without bothering to change the title, which refers to a previous message. If you receive an e-mail entitled 'Re: meeting on 4 November' and you open it to find it's about the follow-up meeting on 5 December, are you likely to be impressed? Or what if you are looking for an audit trail for what happened at the meeting on 5 December? Will you really expect the information in someone's e-mail header of 'Meeting on 4 November'? We think not!

If this strikes a chord with you, adapt so that you don't irritate your readers – or show yourself as disorganized. You'll soon get into the habit, and it will make things much easier for all concerned. Correctly signposted headers also make multicultural e-mail exchanges less challenging. It's complicated enough to read and write business English as a non-native speaker, without the extra hassle of working out what the e-mail is about.

So take the time to choose meaningful subject headings for e-mails. For example, '*Project A: update, end of Week 30*' means more, at a glance, than simply '*Project A*'. In subsequent e-mails, refresh the headings so your writing always reflects the current picture.

Some companies suggest you write alongside each subject heading whether the e-mail requires *reply* or *action* or is purely for *information*. Does your organization require this?

Before you send

- Reread your e-mail and check that it's correct on every level.
- Make sure that it doesn't include previous e-mail threads or chains which may not be appropriate to forward on to the new readers.
- Have you included any attachments you've mentioned?
- If you have copied somebody in, have you explained why?
- Is the subject heading informative and apt?
- Is the e-mail easy to read (in terms of font, size, structure, layout, etc)?

After sending

- Check after the event (a day, two days, a week: in short whatever timeframe applies) that you've achieved the outcome you want. It will help you design your writing better for next time if it didn't work.
- Know where you have filed the e-mail (if you need to keep it). Well-designed writing will help you.

Cc

Cc (carbon copy) is for when you send an e-mail to someone and copy in other recipients, so they see the message. If you use a cc internally within your company, it's not generally a problem when those listed see others' e-mail addresses. But where your cc field includes the e-mail addresses of external recipients, you may get into trouble because of privacy and data protection laws.

It's also important to realize that some businesses filter e-mail so that cc copies are filed separately and only reviewed periodically, for example once a week. So cc may not be the best approach if you need someone to read your e-mail as soon as possible.

Even when you are sure it's appropriate to copy someone in on an e-mail, it's still good to tell them the reason why. You could give some indication after the addressee's name, for example 'To: John Smith (for action)' or 'To: Henk Dreesman (for information)'. Or you could give some indication within your e-mail, for example:

FROM: tarakahmed02@mailink.cn
TO: paulalopez08@mailink.cn
CC: hoileung09@mailink.cn
SUBJECT: Preparation for Board Meeting on 4 March

Hi Paula,
Please find attached the agenda for this meeting. Can I confirm that you will be attending the entire meeting?
Hoi, Please can you confirm that you have been able to give Paula the update she needs for this meeting?
With thanks and kind regards,
Tarak Ahmed

If you don't explain why people are copied in, recipients often wonder:

- Why is this being copied to me?
- Do I need to respond?
- Or is it just the person to whom it is addressed (the addressee) who needs to respond?
- Or is it intended just for information, for one or both of us?

In a global context, there can be cultural implications too. As you're seeing by now, people from some cultures might feel embarrassed or puzzled if they are copied in. They might feel: 'Have I done something wrong?' unless you explain why their name is there. Can you think of anything else that might affect your culture, or cultures with which you do business?

Bcc

Bcc stands for blind carbon copy. It's a copy of an e-mail message sent to a recipient whose address cannot be seen by other recipients. This method is sometimes useful for confidentiality.

How poorly written e-mails can undermine performance

Getting things done fast might not mean doing things well. One thing is very clear: readers often complain about sloppy and mistake-riddled e-mails. As it's important to maintain a quality professional image in corporate communication, Chapter 13 will give you tips on this.

We mentioned in Chapter 5 that some companies suggest a two-minute delay before hitting the 'Send' button. This can work well on two levels. First, it gives staff time to reread what they have written to check for mistakes – because speed can trip us all into making them. Second, it gives staff time to think through whether they are saying what they mean to say.

It's a costly problem when people send e-mails without sufficiently thinking through the end result they seek. It may be easier to fire off e-mails a few times a day to the same recipient, rather than draw the strands together into a structured entity. But is it *efficient*? Is it *green*? Disorganized writing is not energy efficient. Word power used well, on the other hand, saves human resources, time and money, and pleases readers at the same time.

Activity

Look at these three e-mail extracts sent by one person to one of his customers over a period of one hour.

---

1. Subject: Our invoice for purchase number 123

Please find our invoice attached for the services provided.

2. Subject: Our invoice for purchase number 123

Regarding my earlier e-mail, forgot to attach the invoice, sorry about that. I attach it now.

3. Subject: Our invoice for purchase number 123

We would like to thank you very much for your custom and hope to be of continuing service to you in the future.

Activity

Can you jot down your views on sight of this e-mail trail? Can you suggest ways of improving the communication?

_____

_____

_____

_____

_____

_____

Wouldn't *one* carefully thought-through e-mail have been better? The writer would have used his time better by realizing the business message in e-mail three was, from the customer's perspective, of equal importance to the message in e-mail one. The way he has sent it, it appears not only to be disjointed and unstructured, but also to be an after-thought.

The writer also made a mistake hitting the send button too quickly, without checking the attachment was there. Oh, you may say, that's just human error. And yes, we all omit attachments sometimes. But it's an error that still irritates recipients, because it wastes their time if they have to chase up.

Direct cultures might tell you so. And we've heard some bosses react angrily with 'Don't waste my time!' Recipients in an indirect culture may not actually express this, but they may be *thinking* it. And when it comes to writing e-mails, you need to understand the individual personality too. People with tentative personalities or cultures may check progress every hour or so. They need affirmation – but this may irritate those with confident personalities. However, they may be over-confident that e-mails have got through when they haven't.

The trouble is that, ultimately, business deals can be lost or targets missed when e-mails go astray, and if nobody bothers to carry out an audit trail when replies suddenly dry up. Taking time to check is likely to work best in a global context. Once more, we see how writing global English might need the local splash of colour added or subtracted, to ensure that each e-mail works.

Passing e-mails on isn't the end of the story

Here's a scenario common to many companies today. When faced with a problem, colleague A writes an e-mail highlighting the concern to colleague B. Colleague A hits the send button, and imagines the matter will now be settled by colleague B.

But colleague A is making an assumption. And assuming facts is never a good idea in business communication. After writing the e-mail, colleague A needs to follow through, to check that colleague B has the solution and has dealt with the matter. Only then is colleague A's input really over, if the writing task is to be effective.

Even if you press 'Delete', e-mails can come back to haunt you

Even if you think you've deleted e-mails, receivers may have printed them and use them as evidence (even against you). People have lost jobs over this; matters have sometimes gone to litigation too. Have you ever come across this?

Common traps can trip you up when you write e-mails, despite your best intentions. Here are some:

- Speed can make you make mistakes: in meaning, spelling or grammar – especially if English is not your first language.

- Reacting too quickly may mean you don't write a fully considered reply and there may be far-reaching consequences that you should have anticipated.

- Replying in the heat of the moment may mean you write things you regret.

- Failing to understand that e-mail is not conversation (although it may seem that way) can mean you use English idiom, nuances or irony that aren't appropriate for e-mails. Your readers may misunderstand or even be offended.

Instant text messaging

The amazingly fast-growing use of text or other instant messaging demonstrates its ease and popularity. Yet how useful is it as corporate communication generally?

If guidelines are not set, businesses can find text abbreviations assimilated into their previously more formal business writing. As we've discussed, many readers react negatively to overly casual e-mails, so it's likely they will object to this too. And those who don't object to the informality may still have a problem, for example in understanding the meaning.

Let's take another real-life example of a work-related text message: 'con.call.tom.' What does this mean? It's an instant message but that doesn't mean it's instantly clear. Is it for someone called Con to call Tom? Or is Tom on a conference call?

The writer actually meant it as shorthand-reminder to a colleague: 'there will be a conference call tomorrow'. It was sent by a non-native English speaker to an English recipient. He was confused as to what it meant, as he would not have used those abbreviations. So, if he was confused, then non-native English receivers might be even more puzzled. Once again, speed is not the prime driver of efficiency: *sending messages that people understand is*. Criticisms readers make tend to fall into these categories:

- The meaning of English text abbreviations should be clear.

- Text-speak can create barriers just as other jargon does. Unless you use it specifically for those in a target audience who you know appreciate it and comprehend it (such as some social media platforms) readers often complain it's another way of implying (even if unintentionally) 'You don't understand this? Well, you're not in my club!'.

- Text-speak (particularly when transferred into other writing modes) may demonstrate a slackening in quality and professionalism. It implies that anything goes.

Multilingual and other e-mail threads

Would you agree that there's nothing more frustrating, confusing or even downright rude than someone e-mailing you something you really can't understand? And yet it happens daily in multinational organizations, when we find business English intermixed with other languages.

Read the following e-mail chain starting from e-mail 1 at the bottom to e-mail 4 at the top, to see how a multilingual thread can lead to confusion.

E-mail 4 in thread

FROM: nadjagross09@mailink.com
TO: hansbrugman08@mailink.com; petersmith07@mailink.com
SUBJECT: Project X Meeting

Hi Hans und Peter,
Das Meeting findet morgen um halb zwei Uhr nachmittag statt.
Bis morgen.
beste Grüße
Nadja

E-mail 3 in thread

FROM: hansbrugman08@mailink.com
TO: nadjagross09@mailink.com
SUBJECT: Project X Meeting

Hi Nadja,
Wann ist das Meeting morgen? Können Sie bitte auch Peter Smith
Bescheid geben?
Vielen Dank und beste Grüße
Hans

E-mail 2 in thread

FROM: hansbrugman08@maillink.com
TO: petersmith07@maillink.com
SUBJECT: Project X Meeting

Hi Peter,
I'll have to check myself. I'll ask Nadja to let you know, as she is also
going to the meeting.
Kind regards,
Hans

E-mail 1 in thread

FROM: petersmith07@maillink.com
TO: hansbrugman08@maillink.com
SUBJECT: Project X Meeting

Hi Hans,
Please can you confirm what time the meeting is tomorrow?
Thanks and kind regards,
Peter

If you speak German and English, this thread is easy. If you don't, you'll
be puzzled. Naturally, in a global context, we can substitute any other
language for the German component here.

The point is universal. If you work with multinational teams or in an
intercultural working environment and you use e-mail threads, you'll find
this type of scenario commonplace. Peter, in the example, writes in
English. Hans writes in English to Peter and German to Nadja. He asks
Nadja, in German, what time the meeting will be held and asks her to let
Peter know. Nadja replies to Hans' request and copies Peter in to this

message, as requested. She has written, in German, when the meeting is, 'ticked that box,' sent friendly greetings and generally complied with Hans' request, hasn't she?

But it's not actually enough is it, if Peter doesn't understand German? What do you think might happen next? Here are some possibilities that we can think of:

- Peter tries to work out what Nadja has written and gets it right – but wishes he hadn't had to 'decode' the message.

- Peter tries to work out what Nadja has written and gets it wrong. This might be because the German way of expressing time varies from that used in many other countries. 'Half two' is the literal English translation of the German 'halb zwei'. So an online translation may have helped for the number – but the German expression means 1.30 pm not 2.30 pm. (There's more on this in Chapter 14.)

- Peter has no idea what Nadja has written. He is not impressed, as he has to go back to Hans, Nadja or someone else for clarification.

Interestingly, senders are rarely aware that they are causing confusion, embarrassment or even alienating receivers by using these threads. They are often the most helpful colleagues face to face. But because they are able to think and write in more than one language can mean that they *assume* others can too.

To avoid unintended problems, you could try these alternatives:

- Avoid multilingual threads altogether and start each message afresh.

- Consider stopping your multilingual e-mail threads sooner rather than later, maybe after the third message in a row. It's one way of keeping an eye on the situation.

- If a thread is unavoidable, for an audit trail for example, be courteous and efficient by regularly summarizing the main points of the thread in English.

Finally, be aware your e-mail threads may be forwarded to recipients who are not party to the entire thread.

A corporate e-mail policy can help

There are subjects that are generally considered 'off limit' in e-mail and text messages. A corporate policy can help staff realize whether their e-mails (or other written messages) must avoid, for example:

- referring to age, disability, sexual, racial, religious or ethnic topics, which may be considered to be discriminatory in nature;

- referring to anything that could potentially be classed as libel or defamatory in any way, or otherwise lead to legal action against the employer as well as the individual;

- breaking bad news, if another medium might be more tactful.

Does your company have such a policy? If so, is it issued to all staff when they join the organization? Policies usually cover these sorts of question:

- Is e-mail our preferred mode of corporate communication or corporate writing?

- Do we have a corporate style, format, font, point size (plus other points mentioned in Chapter 2)?

- If so, might we ever need to vary this style when we write to a specific audience, in view of differing cultural expectations?

- Are there subjects that are always 'off limit' in e-mail? If so, what are these? Or are there subjects that are sometimes 'off limit' according to the cultural expectations of those in the audience? If so, what are these subjects?

- Are staff encouraged to ask for help when they are not sure about their business English?

- What do we do when we see that people are making mistakes when writing English for business?

- Do we have an induction handbook that sets these points out?

Activity

Are there any other topics you feel should be covered? Or are there any issues about e-mail that you want to record here, for future reference?

_____

_____

_____

_____

_____

_____

Writing effective e-mails gets 'brand you' noticed

If you follow all the tips in this chapter, it's a very good way of being **smart** and **sophisticated** in your global business English communication.

If you are **clear** and you send out structured e-mails to achieve business objectives, if you always check your writing is **comprehensible**, e-mail is a great way of projecting a totally professional image. This stands 'brand you' in good stead.

We've talked about the nuts and bolts of e-mail writing in this chapter, but it's also key to realize that e-mail is, in a sense, one of the first writing modes to give everyone in the organization a voice. The more junior people in an office can get their views in front of more senior people via e-mail threads or address lists. For some cultures or hierarchical organizations, this is quite groundbreaking. People who may never have been seen or heard by the boss can suddenly use written word power skills to make themselves known – and impress if they get it right. We'll pick up on this in Chapter 12 because social media is even more about giving everyone a voice – and opportunities to present 'brand you'.

So, to summarize, capitalize on the fact that so many competitors are prepared to give away their competitive advantage through their sloppy e-mails. They get noticed too – but for all the wrong reasons! You can get noticed for all the *right* reasons, by asking yourself, before you send:

- Is e-mail the right communication medium?
- Would it be a problem for you, or for your organization, if your e-mail was forwarded to other people without your knowledge?

- Have you overreacted, or gone the extra length to anticipate (and answer) further questions?
- Have you run spelling, punctuation and grammar checks on the document (in the correct variety of English)?
- Have you developed the right rapport for your readers and their business and cultural expectations?
- Have you checked your meanings and your objectives?
- Are you sending the attachments promised?
- If you are copying someone in, have you explained why?

Worksheet

Section A: Knowing your theory

Based on what you have understood from this chapter, respond to the following questions and statements by ticking the 'Yes' or 'No' boxes.

	Yes	No
1 Has business e-mail become a preferred medium of communication?	☐	☐
2 Should there be a balance between formal and friendly tones when we write business e-mails?	☐	☐
3 Does it matter if your business e-mail has several spelling and punctuation mistakes?	☐	☐
4 Is having a corporate e-mail policy usually useful?	☐	☐
5 Writing relevant subject headings for business e-mails is a waste of time.	☐	☐
6 Reviewing a business e-mail before you send it is a good way to avoid miscommunication.	☐	☐
7 Readers automatically understand why they have been copied into an e-mail conversation.	☐	☐
8 In a global audience, everybody will be able to understand any abbreviations you use in business e-mails and instant messages, without explanation.	☐	☐

Section B: The business of e-mails

In this chapter, you have learned about the dangers involved in using e-mail as a medium for business communications, and the caution needed in order to write business e-mails as effectively as possible.

As with all forms of business documentation (letters, reports, presentations, social networking media inputs, etc), being **clear**, **comprehensible** and **confident** as well as being **smart** and **sophisticated** are qualities that are also required when you write business e-mails.

In the following exercise, first identify the errors in this e-mail.

TO: MaryP@group5services.net
CC: Paul.Bennetton@BestAccountancy.com

Hey Mary,
We've noticed that you'd never sent us back that invoice we sent you in july!
Can you find it, sign it and send it 2 us asap plz?
Cheers, ☺
Paul.
Paul Benetton,
Chief Accountant
www.BestAccountancy.com

Now rewrite this e-mail here:

TO: MaryP@group5services.net
CC: Paul.Bennetton@BestAccountancy.com

Chapter Seven
Making an impact

Don't assume your readers are interested in what you write. Make what you write interesting. Word power helps.

The 'wow factor' sets you apart

Great writing can help you make your mark and set you apart from the rest. After all, nobody ever made it to the top by blending in, did they? And the wow factor can be as simple as words that stand out from the page.

Impact can have staying power too. That's something that's hard to harness in today's attention-deficient world. Whatever we write, the minute we press the 'Send' button, or post our letter, or print out our report, the present changes into the past in the blink of an eye. 'Next' – the power of the new – can be seen to have more currency. That's the perception, whether right or wrong. If our words make the right impact, they have much more power to leap into the future.

It's true that culture often determines whether we shout out or whisper our talents and wares. However, it's pretty much a universal truth that people rarely achieve their goals by being 'a well-kept secret'.

Powerful descriptions sell better

For practical examples of how impact sells 'better than bland', let's look at the world of online auctions, a key feature in the digital age. Let's take two separate sellers, each with one of two identical brand new CDs to sell. Seller 1 lists the CD's title, spells it wrongly and sets out its price. Seller 2 lists the CD's title, mentions the fact it's brand new and 'one of the most eagerly awaited CDs' of the year. Every detail is correct and the whole listing professionally set out. The CD is listed at a considerably higher price than seller 1's.

You may think the price that undercuts the rest will win each time – but it's not always so. Readers often view a listing that's peppered with mistakes or incorrect in other ways, as describing a bootleg or second-hand product, even though the item may well be new and authentic. The quality of the description very often affects credibility – of the product and of the person who has written the description.

For instance, you may be looking for Louis Vuitton leather goods. You see three identical travel bags listed. The written description of the first is *Louis Vuitton*, the second is *Luis Vuitton*, the third is *Louis Viutton*. On the basis that the second and third spellings are wrong, you may, rightly or wrongly, suspect the bags in those listings are counterfeit. Even if the first seller is asking a higher price, you may be prepared to pay it because you think it's more likely to be genuine. Cheaper price may not be the determining factor as to why you buy, surprising as this may be.

Amazingly, on occasion, a listing with 'power wording' will sell for as much as double the price. The more expensive the product the greater this effect is, because people will often pay a premium for what they see as the right quality. Power words can reinforce this perception. Indeed, the Louis Vuitton Group doesn't just promote the brand as 'leather goods': it conveys added value in the description 'luxury leather goods'.

We'll stay with the theme of online auction sites. Does it surprise you that even when it comes to buying large specialist items, a written description may be the most important aspect that a potential buyer has to focus on?

Let's say a business has a power generator to sell online. The company has potential buyers who aren't going to be able to try the generator out to see if it works. They may be unable to find a product test or review. So, imagine those prospective purchasers have narrowed it down to two models sold by two different sellers. The models are very similar. In fact a buyer may suspect they were made at the same factory, under differing brand names. It happens. Yet the price difference between the two could be as much as 300 per cent.

Seller 1 has posted a picture and price. Seller 2 has added a description using power words or phrases such as 'state of the art', 'reliable', 'guaranteed,' 'rapid dispatch' and 'after-purchase advice'. This makes the product stand out and engage buyers' attention. A good written description in accessible English can sell better.

Words can create a following

Well-chosen words can create a following for you. Because of the digital age, 'following' is a term that has even more meaning attached to it today than in the past. Twitter and other social media are clear testimony to that, as we show in Chapter 12. If people follow where you lead, it helps you develop sustainable business relationships with them.

If you are selling and your communication aligns with your target audience's values, even if those people do not buy from you now, there's every chance they may be more likely to buy from you in the future. What's more, if they have already bought from you and liked what you provided, they may ask you to develop your range. All things being equal, you prefer to stay with people you understand, like and trust, don't you? It does seem to be a universal truth across cultures.

Word power skills

You don't have to be a marketing professional to know that in business your words must appeal to your target audience. You need to grab people's attention and get them actively 'in the loop' (also commonly referred to in business as 'consumer engagement and involvement').

How do you do this? You could start by identifying which business words – out of the thousands you may come across each day – make the most positive impact on you. Sometimes we really like words that others use, without realizing we too can use these, or similar words to take our businesses forward. Just because your organization may have used the same wording (for example in templates) over the years, doesn't mean you shouldn't suggest change, if change would help. Creative design agencies don't have a monopoly on innovation, do they?

So look at the world around you with fresh eyes. Actively comparing others' styles of writing can help you identify what works. Here's an example.

> A colleague booked two holidays, each with a different travel company. Each operator sent a letter of confirmation with a separate heading as follows:
>
> Subject heading used by travel company 1: IT'S ALL BOOKED!
> Subject heading used by travel company 2: Confirmation of booking

If you compare the two subject headings, can you see a clear difference in tone between the two? The second is 'flatter' than the first: it has less enthusiasm. It is perfectly acceptable but maybe many readers will prefer the vitality expressed in the first heading.

How do you react to this? Personality and culture will play a part. But we also need to ensure that the language we use resonates with readers. When you choose which variety of English to use, you can still harness your own values, as we've seen. But you may have to work out how to align these with your target readers' values and expectations.

Let's go back to the travel companies' subject headings. The 'etiquette' for written business English is normally to avoid writing in upper case (capital) letters, in e-mails at least. Many readers equate this with SHOUTING. Even if we think this convention should be avoided in letters too, most of us wouldn't mind, would we, if we see writers who 'shout' with apparent happiness, as is the case here? They seem pleased because their client's holiday has been successfully arranged. Wouldn't we be happy too?

It is absolutely true that travel company 2 has chosen a heading that is fit for purpose. But compared to the other company's headline it can seem 'overcautious' and may ultimately create problems. Can you see why?

We can think of at least two reasons. The first is that travel company 2 could possibly come across as uninterested in what it does and in its clients. If this is the case, then it may ultimately lose out to competitors who go out of their way to show they are pleased when things go right for their clients.

There's nothing wrong in either of the two written examples we've just examined. Our hearts as well as our minds often come into the equation though. In one scenario, our eyes see writing that expresses a company is delighted to have the opportunity to help with our travel arrangements and wishes us well. If we sense with our emotions that the sentiments expressed are sincere, we rather like it.

Maybe the other company – who, by comparison, is simply efficient with no frills – is starting to look slightly less attractive. In our minds, we may downgrade their good performance to 'satisfactory' and may upgrade the enthusiastic company's good performance to 'excellent'. That's the effect word power can have.

Only harness the level of enthusiastic word power that in the final analysis sits with who you are, with your culture and what you do. Everywhere in the world, readers see through insincerity. Never be false in your communication; always respect your audience. This is one way your global English can indeed be used as universal currency.

We routinely ask attendees at workshops to tell us the power words they find have a particularly strong impact and are effective. They invariably include some of these words and phrases:

- you, we;
- free, advice without cost, value for money, low cost, cost-effective;
- success, successful;
- now, immediate, fast, today;
- easy, efficient, effective;
- benefits, advantages, results;
- help, support, integrity;
- expert, expertise, professional, professionalism, know-how;
- latest, breakthrough, world first;
- best, excellence, first class, totally professional;
- quality, authenticity;
- safe, green, eco-friendly, energy efficient, welfare, security;
- valued, valuable;
- please, thank you;
- premier, outstanding, unrivalled, unsurpassed, inspirational;

- remarkable, passionate, talented, amazing, exciting, awesome;
- total, complete, integrated solution, assurance;
- friendly, personable, caring, respectful;
- trustworthy, reliable, reassuring, responsible;
- well informed, up to date, ahead of the times.

These come over as positive words and phrases and it's hardly surprising people like these best. Some are very traditional (for example 'assurance'), some are reserved (such as 'respectful'), and others are effusive (for example 'awesome') – so ultimately some may appeal more to one culture than another.

Sometimes, however, negative sounding words and phrases also have a strong impact and are powerful in a business context. Here are some examples:

- Can you afford not to? (Then you go on to highlight a problem for which you or your company has a solution.)
- Ignore this at your peril!
- Don't take the risk.
- Eliminate your problems.
- Why struggle with the hassle?

Activity

Which power words would be right for your culture – or perhaps for the differing cultures of those in your target audience? If you write for subcultures (as we mentioned in Chapter 1) maybe some words wouldn't be right for some personalities. Jot down your thoughts here.

_____

_____

_____

_____

_____

_____

There's food for thought here. Choose the ingredients – the right words – then add the right seasoning, so to speak, to serve up the right impact. You might find it useful to ask colleagues for help in getting the overall recipe right!

Also, don't forget that manners can make impact. Once again, you need to understand the culture of the people with whom you are communicating but it is almost a universal truth that bad manners will get you noticed for the wrong reasons; good manners for the right. Be **sophisticated** and **confident**.

Who takes centre stage?

To make the best connections with readers, you might find that you need to adjust your communication so that the spotlight is not just on you. When the lights, camera, action roll, (so to speak) maybe you need to let readers take centre stage.

It's good to visualize things from time to time. Express images in your writing to add vitality. The world of film or show business is often used in business advertising for this reason, for product endorsement. Companies find that spoken and written slogans can engage audience buy-in by implying that celebrities' buying power gives them access to 'the best choices available'. If products are 'good enough for celebrities' then they are going to be good for the rest of us too.

Are there any such advertisements in your region? Here's one example that has international currency:

CASE STUDY   L'Oréal

For many years now, global cosmetics company L'Oréal's advertising for its products has been focusing on endorsements from celebrities. Originally, the endorsement as to why the star the company features at any given time had used a particular product was 'because I'm worth it'.

Over years, the company has stayed with the celebrity theme, but changed the slogan along these lines: '(buy this) because you're worth it' and also: '(buy this) because 'we (originally women, though now L'Oréal has expanded its market to include men too) are worth it'. The company has neatly converted the (self-preoccupied) 'I' of the celebrity, to the inclusive 'you' and 'we' that includes a massive, potential global audience.

Let's just look again at those two words 'you' and 'we'. Do you remember where they featured on the list of powerful words that people tell us carry most weight for them? Right at the top: that's how important they are.

Be aware that celebrity-based endorsement has to be meaningful for your target audience. It's highly visible in India, parts of Asia and the West. But it isn't appreciated in the same way everywhere. In fact, where a celebrity culture may not be relevant, it could actually annoy, even alienate, your audience.

Here's another internationally available product: professional indemnity insurance, a must for most businesses. Have you got it? If you have, what do you look for in your policy?

We bet excitement is not top of your list. Yet one insurance company sent a letter inviting business owners to buy its '*exciting new product*' (its latest professional insurance). So yes, a power word ('exciting') has been used – but is it really the right word for the target market? Are we enthused by a product that we buy of necessity? It's never going to be on anyone's 'wish-list of nice things to have', is it?

So we weren't surprised in the least when a second letter came out some months later from this company. The word 'exciting' had been ditched. The new strapline read along the following lines:

> '*Does it concern you that there are many things you can be sued for in business? Well, worry no longer: our comprehensive new policy is designed to provide you peace of mind.*'

This time, the message resonated with its audience by highlighting why businesses need insurance. It mentioned a very real problem and it offered a solution. It used negative word power to make readers feel (justifiably) nervous but redressed the balance by offering *peace of mind*. That has universal currency. It worked.

Build up a dossier of good examples and serve your customers well

Word power isn't just about vitality of expression. It also helps us communicate the right attitudes. Sometimes you can express reader or customer focus simply by avoiding elements that don't express it! These can be negative elements such as:

- being prepared to let readers see spelling or grammatical errors as your company norm;
- writing the wrong words in the wrong place, at the wrong time;
- conveying the wrong sentiments, such as 'don't', 'can't' and 'won't'.

If we don't filter out such things, we might unknowingly build up an impression that we don't care. So try to create a 'we do care' scenario wherever you can.

One easy way is to focus on what you like to see, as a consumer. It's easy because companies compete for your attention every day. Whether it's through customized mail; impersonal junk mail; advertisements online, on television, in newspapers or magazines; businesses are relying on readers to become consumers. And as consumers, we all have opinions on which business communication works well, fairly well and so on, right down to the stuff that's abysmal in our estimation – the type that annoys and alienates those it should be attracting and supporting.

In the worksheet at the end of this chapter we're going to ask you to create a dossier of writing from the world around you, to see what works and what doesn't, in your opinion. Once you have done this, you are likely to find that what makes a message work or not depends on many features, including:

- the vocabulary used;
- the accuracy of the words and grammar;
- the clarity of the message;
- its appropriateness;
- the attitude conveyed and the tone used;

- the colours and the font used;
- the layout;
- the images or lack of them.

Enjoy being a style detective! Ditch techniques that fail; identify what's likely to work for readers and serve them well.

Standard written endings can wreck impact

Most cultures appreciate the personal touch in customer service. Whether that personal touch is high impact and expressive, or lower impact and understated, customers generally prefer a company to treat them as people, not numbers.

That's why most companies today understand the real need to develop good customer relations, sometimes referred to as customer relationship management (CRM). It's one reason why many call-centres have thrown away the tight scripts they used to use on unsolicited cold calls. We can all hear insincerity when we come across it.

But we can still find the 'autopilot' approach 'alive and unwell' in many companies' written communications. An example can be the routine use of standard endings to letters or e-mails. In business, the term 'standard ending' generally refers to the written sentence that appears before the writer's signature, to signify that the letter or e-mail is drawing to a close.

Here are some common examples of standard endings:

- I look forward to hearing from you.
- Please feel free to contact me for further details.
- Please don't hesitate to call if there's further information that would help.
- We await your further instructions in the matter.
- We trust you find this information helpful.

Standard endings may be right for routinely acknowledging a letter, for example: 'We will give your letter the attention it deserves and get back to you shortly.' But readers the world over tell us that some standard endings wreck tone and impact. Even when companies had the best intentions, the standard ending used can incense readers – and can even be seen as customer disservice.

So why is this a common problem in global business English? It's because writers often extract standard expressions from textbooks or from online discussion forums, and fail to check or customize how they use them.

Some time ago, consumers bought a new washing machine made by a leading manufacturer. Many were shocked to find that their washing was getting torn by the machine. They wrote to the manufacturer – and no doubt this is what they expected to hear back:

1 A prompt, interim acknowledgement of their complaints, if not a full reply by return.

2 Some expression of empathy: 'We are sorry to hear about the problems' (whether or not the manufacturer was accountable).

3 An indication that someone from the company would arrange a follow-up inspection to investigate the situation (people's washing was being ruined, after all) and to put things right.

Here is a real-life standard ending to a letter that the company sent to disgruntled customers:

I am sorry to hear about the damage caused to your clothes during washing, but your (named brand) washing machine model has complied with all our standard checks.

I trust you find this information helpful.

The Manager
Customer Care Department
(Company name)

Can you imagine how customers felt on receiving this? They were already displeased; this reply made them angrier. Consumers banded together to publicize the fault via a national television programme that championed consumers' rights. It transpired there was indeed a problem with the machines' interior mechanism, which the manufacturer had to replace, at no cost to their customers.

The physical repairs naturally cost the company money, but what about the cost to its reputation? Bad news travels fast. So, wouldn't it have been better to have responded more personally from the outset, with a better and non-standard ending to their letter? They would have served customers better and provided some level of damage limitation.

Activity

Do you use standard endings in your organization? If so, are there any that you think should be reviewed in the light of this chapter? Are there any standard endings that other companies use that annoy you? Jot down your thoughts here.

_____

_____

_____

_____

_____

_____

So, writing with impact can emerge from surprising circumstances, not just positive experiences. Companies who are honest enough to admit when something has gone wrong can actually hit the right chord. It may not be the impact they originally hoped for, but readers may actually appreciate their openness and honesty. What readers don't appreciate is when a company is overly preoccupied with procedures (for example 'the product met our safety standards') and does not focus, as it should, on alleviating any bad experiences consumers suffer. If we are truly to deliver customer service, we need to express this in any writing we send, for example 'We're really sorry about the problems this caused you.'

This is another important aspect of writing with impact and one that applies to all levels of business writing, across all cultures.

Worksheet

Section A: Knowing your theory

Based on what you have understood from this chapter, respond to the following questions and statements by ticking the 'Yes' or 'No' boxes.

		Yes	No
1	Is it true that a written description of a product is still important today?	☐	☐
2	Are the values of your target audience unimportant when it comes to attracting business?	☐	☐
3	Can you sometimes use negative-sounding words and phrases to make impact in business communications?	☐	☐
4	Word power matters in consumer engagement.	☐	☐
5	Can overuse of negative words such as 'don't', 'can't', and 'won't' put off customers?	☐	☐
6	Few cultures appreciate the personal touch in customer service.	☐	☐
7	It's important to customize templates taken from online and other sources.	☐	☐
8	Do you need to make sure your business English reflects sincerity (that is, it shows that you and your company truly care)?	☐	☐

Section B: Communicating with impact

This chapter focuses on how to make an impact in the way you use and write global business English. It's about how to gain your target audience's interest and enduring engagement. We want you to see that everyone can develop the impact factor when they write. Even the most complex technical report can 'wow' when structured with impact and written with style and enthusiasm.

So, have you ever thought of creating a dossier of writing from the world around you, to see what works and what doesn't, in your opinion? It doesn't have to be from your work environment: it can be anything at all that is related to business. It's like the 'show and tell' you might have done at primary school – made 'grown-up' in a business context.

Once you have collected enough examples for a pattern to emerge, jot down the features that worked, as well as the features that didn't work.

Try to do this on a continuing basis.

Chapter Eight
Using the global word power skills guide

"Writing is absolutely not just about putting pen to paper or typing out a message. It can be a science as much as an art.

What is the global word power skills guide?

This is a four-step guide that brings many of our tips together, to help you write global business English effectively on a daily basis. People tell us it helps with spoken skills as well. It works like this:

Step 1: Be correct for purpose

- Know what your writing needs to achieve, alongside what your company needs to achieve.
- Match readers' or customers' expectations at the very least.
- Make sure you are using the right communication medium for your objectives.
- Make sure your writing does not contain mistakes.
- Your business communication will fail if you get your basics wrong.

Step 2: Be clear and comprehensible

- Use accessible English and express facts simply, wherever possible.
- Edit well so your main points are easy to see and understand.
- Make sure you are using the right business English language for your target audience.

Confused messages undermine your objectives. They can lose you custom too.

Step 3: Be smart and sophisticated – and make the right impact

- Use the right words and style to get noticed for the right reasons.
- Understand how to project 'brand you' alongside your company brand.
- Understand when to 'use a splash of local colour' (either your own or your target audience's, if different).
- Write to create opportunities.

Step 4: Focus on your readers

- Use plain English.
- Be aware of differing personalities' and cultural expectations; write from your readers' perspectives as well as your own, wherever possible; empathize.
- Use positive, proactive words where possible, such as those shown in Chapter 7.
- Use words that are relevant for your target audience.

Follow these steps for successful written communications.

Being correct for purpose

Being correct for purpose (Step 1) is about identifying why you write in business. You have to decide your communication objectives and the locality of your target audience, before you decide the variety of business English you use, as we demonstrated in principle in Chapters 1 and 2. We're now going to develop this theme, using the system we've shown.

CASE STUDY

The sales director of a manufacturing company had a meeting with a valued client, Mr Prakash Patel. As a follow-up, he needed to write an e-mail itemizing points they had agreed. This was the primary purpose of his communication. So, on one level, he would be 'correct for purpose' in writing:

> 'Dear Mr. Patel, I am writing to confirm below the points we agreed at our meeting last week...' before going on to record what those points were.

Beyond this, the sales director decided he could develop a parallel secondary purpose – and take the concept 'correct for purpose' to a level beyond this primary purpose. His writing could create an opportunity to sustain the good working relationship that the two had already developed.

So he discarded the opening sentence set out in the first paragraph, and instead began his e-mail:

> 'Dear Mr. Patel, It was really good meeting you again last week. We really value your custom, so I'm pleased to agree to your points as follows...'

and proceeded to write down the agreed items, ending with a cordial greeting.

In expressing to Mr Patel the fact that he is valued, the message has become more personalized. This is a must for some cultures. Is it for yours? And some businesses and cultures would have swapped the e-mail greeting 'Dear Mr Patel' for 'Hi Prakash' as we have seen in earlier chapters. Would yours?

Being correct has a third meaning in this section as well. It's about checking your business writing is free of mistakes before you issue it. This is as important for native English writers as for non-native writers, as readers often make an instant value judgement: mistakes equal lack of professionalism.

What's more, lack of professionalism in communication may reflect poor products or service, in readers' eyes anyway. We've already referred to this in online auctions, as one example. In Chapters 12 and 13 we'll deal further with how readers make that relentless 'instant evaluation of quality'. They do it now, in the digital era, more than ever before, as your written errors can go viral at the click of a button. The days of imagining that mistakes don't matter should be well and truly over!

Write clearly and comprehensibly

Your writing will be **clear** and **comprehensible** (Step 2) when you highlight key messages concisely and your readers understand the meaning you intended. As you've seen earlier in the book, layout can also help writing appear clear. Informative headings, subheadings and short sentences can have the very real advantage of signposting what we say, helping readers navigate.

We cannot stress enough that ease of navigation is something readers increasingly expect as most writing today is web-based. It therefore needs a new, organic structure, no longer based on yesterday's rigid writing structure of beginning, middle and end.

Hold this image of a signpost in your mind. You need to know where your writing is leading so that your readers understand and can follow. This in itself can help you avoid writing too much densely packed material at a go. The moment your readers get lost because they're confused or put off by 'a forest of information overload' or muddled directions is the moment your business communication is likely to fail.

The key to writing successfully today has to be to design interesting text and layout, including varied sentence length, but nothing overly long. If you write sentences containing more than 40 words, you'll find a high proportion of a native audience have to revisit parts in order to check meaning. It's likely to be higher if the people in your audience are non-native English readers. So be fair! If you do have a lot of information to convey, you could try devices such as:

- bullet lists or numbered points to break up the otherwise large chunk of text;

- subheadings in bold, to work as additional points of interest, and also give structure that both helps readers and grabs attention;

- an appendix (or appendices) or electronic document attachments or hyperlinks when the communication is electronic.

Writing simply is not about being simplistic

If people are *quickly able to understand* what you write, you benefit by being able to focus on what really matters: getting your key messages across and reducing the chance of misunderstandings. This is particularly important on websites and in other digital media where people in your audience will actually expect to skim read. They need – and you need them – to get your meaning instantly, if at all possible, before they move on to the next link.

Simple words are most often understood. It's a compelling reason to use them in business – but in the digital era, it's not the only one, as we are going to explain throughout this chapter.

To help develop the habit of choosing the simplest words in English each time, take a look at the following list of words or phrases. We list a more complex word followed by a simpler word with the *same meaning*. So it's not about being simplistic or 'dumbing down' your business English at all.

assist	help
visualize	see
state	say
purchase	buy
sufficient	enough
approximately	about
require	need
in order that	so
statutory	legal
due to the fact that	because

ascertain	check
materialize	happen
supplementary cost	extra cost
competencies	skills

Activity

Can you think of any complex business English words that you, your colleagues or suppliers use that might work better for readers if changed into simpler words? List them here. You may like to swap notes with colleagues too.

_____

_____

_____

_____

_____

_____

Writing for impact

You are **smart** and **sophisticated** and write with impact (Step 3) when you understand the part you personally can play in making a difference through your business writing and other interaction. It's about realizing that using the right words can lift your communication, making the ordinary extraordinary. It can provoke the right feelings about you and your organization in the estimation of the people in your audience. These feelings can in turn lead to the desired action – on your part and on theirs – towards achieving your business and personal goals.

Earlier in the book, we asked you to identify the words that best portray your qualities and how you want readers to see you, as well as your organization. Do you remember the words you jotted down? If not, take a look at them now, alongside the power words you identified in the last chapter.

Don't forget to add the 'local splash of colour' we refer to throughout the book, including all activities and worksheets.

Focus on your readers

You focus on your readers (Step 4) when you try to see things from their perspective when you write. One aid to doing this is to use plain English (known as plain language in the United States), a concept that's well known to native English speakers, but not always to non-native writers. It means *accessible English* that people are likely to understand.

The move towards plain English originated from a consumer backlash against verbosity and pomposity. This was, and is, often associated with bureaucracy, as much legal and public sector documentation is written in language seemingly designed to complicate matters! And if this is true for native English users, imagine the difficulty for those for whom English is a second or third language. So the simple words we have set out above, when discussing Step 2, can play a dual role of being clear, as well as exemplifying plain English and focusing on the readers.

More recent developments in our digital world make an equally pressing case for adopting plain English in order best to serve our readers. Surveys show that, thanks to the ever-growing use of text speak via mobile devices and social networking sites, increasing numbers of people (especially the young) believe that if you use long words, you're out-of-touch with the modern world.

Whereas in the past, people who used more complex vocabulary might have been viewed as 'superior', today they might be seen as being outdated. This fact will surprise people from some cultures more than others. Does it surprise you? Would you agree with an overall view that people who communicate in common language in the workplace, as well as socially, are those with whom more people can relate?

It definitely makes commercial sense for you to check your target audience's stance on this. For example, can you imagine the commercial cost if your websites don't work for you because your vocabulary seems old-fashioned? Your website developer may have come up with the right search engine keywords to drive traffic to your site but once people are there, it's over to you to deliver the right descriptions of your products or services, on every level.

Twitter has also added its global weight to the case of plain English (there's more about Twitter in Chapter 12). Why? Well, if you can't write it in 140 characters or less, you might find yourself out-smarted by someone who can. In the language of this book, simplicity is the new elegance: another, perhaps unexpected, way to be **sophisticated**.

Increasingly, plain English is also about choosing active verb forms over passive ones. Let's explain what we mean. In English, you can express action in a sentence in two ways:

The employee wrote the document.

The document was written by the employee.

The 'active voice' is where the subject *does something*. The first sentence uses the active voice. In the second sentence the subject is the *document* – and it is acted upon or receives the action (from the employee who wrote it).

The meaning is clear enough in these examples. But sometimes use of the passive voice makes things somewhat or even very unclear. For example: '*A decision was taken not to proceed with this proposal.*' This sentence can confuse because readers don't know who took the decision. In a business context, it may be very important that they do. Who do they contact to see what happens next, if anything? Or who should they try to persuade to have a rethink – before turning a deal down, for example? Readers cannot know from the context; they need more information.

Native English speakers may feel confident to ask for that information. They may, however, be annoyed at the writer leaving it out. For non-native English speakers, the passive writing can be an unwanted barrier to understanding the message.

If you use passives too readily, they can make your writing seem old-fashioned; sometimes unintentionally pompous. Not only may it be unclear, as we've mentioned, as to who does what. Passives can make it seem unnecessary for anyone to do anything!

Read this example to see what we mean: '*Consideration should be given as to whether this amount should be calculated as part of the amount outstanding or be passed over to the Finance Department to work out.*' Can you see a lack of ownership and direction right at the beginning of the sentence?

By using the phrase '*consideration should be given*', the writer highlights that something probably should be done, out of two possibilities:

1 either calculating an amount *or*

2 passing the matter to the Finance Department to work out.

But the writer doesn't suggest which of the two options could be the better one to take – or who will decide, and do what needs to be done. So the meaning isn't entirely clear. It's definitely not plain English with focus on the readers.

But there are times when business writers do need to use the passive voice. Occasionally, you need to soften your approach, in this case, to not blame someone directly for something that's gone wrong.

For many Asian cultures, for example, this may be essential. China, Japan and Korea immediately spring to mind as countries where it would be a huge detriment to doing business to cause someone to lose face. And one of the easiest ways to do this would be openly to criticize an individual through the use of the active, for example *'you made a mistake in this calculation'*.

In business, naturally all cultures will on occasion make mistakes – and they will have to be corrected. But to avoid embarrassment (even humiliation) it could be far better, to use the oblique passive: *'There may have been something factored in incorrectly somewhere along the line. It would be good if somebody could check this for us, please.'*

When jargon can lose the focus on readers

Jargon is the name usually given to words or expressions used by a particular profession or group. It can be **clear** and **comprehensible** and fit Step 2 in our system if it uses one word or phrase, rather than many, to sum up something that everyone in the user group understands. Used correctly, it has focus on the readers.

The problem that very often arises, however, is that jargon is used without an initial explanation, as the writer doesn't realize that:

1 in multicultural teams and global settings in particular, the jargon used may not be universally understood;

2 whatever has been written may end up with a wider, perhaps totally unexpected readership, of people who almost certainly will not all understand the jargon.

In the digital age, we must be aware that whatever we write may be read by people we never imagined it would be. Now do you see how jargon that may have started life as perfectly acceptable, without further explanation, may quickly become the problem, not the solution? Once jargon appears on your website, or your article (containing jargon that *seemed right* at the time) appears on *someone else's* online forum for example, it may be too late. Unintentionally – even unknowingly – you may have put up a barrier to future business interaction. So that explanation at the outset makes a great deal of commercial sense.

Before we move on from this topic, there's a new 'kid on the block' too! Online forums regularly get outpourings of resentment against business writers who use 'management speak' or buzz words, commonly seen as the 'new jargon'. Here are some examples of what we mean:

- This is on my radar.
- We need some blue sky thinking.
- Let's reach for the low-hanging fruit.
- Let's push the envelope.
- Leverage yourself to bring your A game to the table.
- Touch base.
- Use your inner passion.
- We're looking for core competencies.

We're not even going to explain what these expressions mean, because that is the whole point. They will mean slightly different things to different people – and if they are in use in your culture, or office subculture and so on, you need to check what they are *supposed* to mean. You can be on tricky ground using them widely, as they are unlikely ever to be universal currency and, in the twinkling of an eye, the new jargon can quickly become yesterday's cast-off.

Acronyms can be a form of jargon too

When you first use an acronym in your written communication, the convention is to write the compound word in full, and put the acronym in brackets after it. For example: World Health Organization (WHO). Subsequently, you can just use the acronym, as readers can understand the meaning.

In practice, however, many writers forget to explain. They write profusely on subjects that readers cannot understand, or try to understand but get the wrong meaning. Take a well-known duplication as an example: the acronym 'WWF'. It can both represent 'World Wildlife

Fund' and also 'World Wrestling Federation'. You can see how that might confuse, depending on a reader's interests!

So using and overusing English acronyms without thought, can be where the business world goes crazy. The moment readers have to ask: 'What does this mean?' (assuming they are confident enough, or their culture allows them to admit they don't know) is when acronyms become a barrier to effective communication.

Activity

Have you come across jargon, including management speak, in business English? If so, are there examples that others use that you don't understand or that annoy you, which you can jot down here?

_____

_____

_____

_____

_____

Do you ever use jargon, including management speak, yourself? Can you jot any down here – and maybe check with a focus group from your target audience that people really do understand it?

_____

_____

_____

_____

_____

Do use the four-step guide as a tool that shows you how to bring together, in every writing task, correctness, clarity, impact and focus on your readers. It's a tool that you'll need increasingly throughout your career. You may think you write a lot at the beginning and in the middle stages of your career, but this skill is something you'll need to develop until you reach the top – and then some more. Believe us, that's the time when staff will copy you in to most things they send out. They'll be looking for you to lead, otherwise how else can they follow?

Activity

To help you bring the steps together in your writing, take a look at this progress report an engineer submitted to his boss by e-mail. Before reading our comments that follow, we would like you to critique it. Could it be better set out and better developed?

FROM: harry@anymail.com
TO: gerhardmendez@anymail.com
SUBJECT: Project

Morning, hope you are well. I understand you were asking for some sort of update on this. Well, here is the production progress made regarding the component sets for the project. The objective is to manufacture 5 units and, as far as I have been able to ascertain, to date 4 have been completed. That said, testing and software is yet to be completed on these. Systems release notes will naturally be generated on completion of the units. I trust this information is helpful and clarifies matters. If not, do let me know if you need any other information and I will amplify further.

What were your findings? Note them here.

_____

_____

_____

_____

_____

_____

Our tips to the engineer would be:

- Write a more precise subject heading to start with. Be correct for purpose. Which project is it? It presumably has a title, so use it.

- Separate the greeting from the progress report. Focus on your reader.

- If you don't have a progress report template, consider developing one simply, with specific signposting, such as: **Current status: work completed and work outstanding** (both itemized), **Risks and issues**, **Ownership**, **Budget status**, etc.

- Do more in terms of focusing on your reader, by explaining what may be ahead of target or what may be slipping and needs extra attention.

- Don't be tentative. Be proactive in anticipating extra questions your boss may ask – before he or she has to.

Worksheet

Section A: Knowing your theory

Based on what you have understood from this chapter, respond to the following questions and statements by ticking the 'Yes' or 'No' boxes.

	Yes	No
1 According to the global word power skills guide, one level of being correct refers to knowing what your writing needs to achieve, alongside what your company needs to achieve.	☐	☐
2 Is it important to write keeping your readers' perspectives in mind?	☐	☐
3 Writing overly-long text keeps things interesting.	☐	☐
4 Writing simply means being simplistic or 'dumbing down' your business English.	☐	☐

	Yes	No
5 Is it always best to avoid the passive voice in writing?	☐	☐
6 In a digital world your jargon may be forwarded on to readers who might not understand it.	☐	☐
7 When first introducing an acronym into your writing, the convention is to write the compound word in full and put the acronym in brackets after it.	☐	☐
8 Keeping subject headings precise helps to set the overall tone of your communication.	☐	☐

Section B: Make your word power skills go global

So, now that you have read the global word power skills guide, here's an exercise for you – a self-assessment of how strong your global word power skills are.

Can you think of some international or cross-cultural issues that currently affect your business? Try to pick an article from *The Financial Times*, the *Economist*, the *Wall Street Journal*, or any other quality, business-based publication in English that covers these issues. Or you might like to go to the BBC website at bbc.co.uk/news.

Read through the article you select and then summarize it in an e-mail (for example to your line manager or team leader) itemizing how the points raised in the article may affect your business or the organization you work for.

In your writing, remember to apply the four-step process shown in the global word power skills guide.

Chapter Nine
Report writing

Making the complex appear easy is a lifetime skill worth developing.

Are your report-writing skills right for today?

In this digital age it's noticeable that global companies are often moving away from formal report writing. In Chapter 4 we highlighted one aspect of this: the fact that presentations are increasingly seen as the new 'global reports'.

We also see the reports of yesteryear frequently replaced by more informal collaborative reviews, sent electronically more often than not. Sometimes these are simply a question of creating an open dialogue which may not even have to lead to a conclusion. Other times, these reviews are – in theory at least – where the main report writer gathers facts and then adds his or her evaluation of these. This may lead to a finished document presenting a business case for consideration.

What we often find in practice is that the 'finished' written document is anything but finished! One of the main reasons for this is because it's very tempting for the report writer just to 'cut and paste' from Word documents that others have e-mailed as their input.

How often have you seen for yourself that 'cut and paste' doesn't necessarily work by itself? Someone has to take ownership for adapting the material to fit the brief. It's not just publishers who need editors – companies need any staff who write to understand how to edit too. Otherwise readers of business reports may see:

- noticeable differences in writing style within the report;
- obvious lack of fluidity in content and argument;
- repetition;
- lack of clear direction;
- conflicting information or recommendations.

Our tip is that, for every business report-writing task, one person needs to take ownership both of the brief (why the report is being written) and also for editing the final document. This is to ensure that all the points made by contributors appear in a logical sequence; topics are differentiated and all recommendations are clearly argued and well thought-through.

So, it's important that you know your organization's stance on reports to know which tips will be relevant. One thing will be constant, however. Whichever style your organization prefers, you'll need to plan your writing stages methodically, including: the background, current position, implications and possibilities; and the main findings and any changes you are recommending.

Have you evaluated your target audience and your role?

As far as you possibly can, identify before you write:

- Why are you writing and who will be your key readers?
- How much do they know about the subject?
- Do they need to use the report? If so, how? For example, do they need it to improve results in areas in which they are accountable? Do they need it so that they are kept informed about others' achievements?
- Are they interested in the report or must you create that interest?
- Must you inform, persuade, cover yourself, anticipate problems and/or offer solutions?
- Do you need to monitor any results and have an ongoing status record?

Checklist: Plan before you write

1 Take time to understand the brief and evaluate the business case, if needed.

2 Check the deadline.

3 Find out who has input alongside yours (if anyone)?

4 Check the relevant background.

5 Understand the target audience and how to write for them.

6 Decide what analysis is needed.

7 Identify what recommendations you or others should make.

8 Draw up your plan.

9 Write the report and evaluate how to make the right impact, distinguishing between:

– the 'essential to know';

– the 'nice to know';

– the 'do not need to know'.

10 By now you are well aware that readers expect brevity in the digital age. But not all reports can be short. It would be wrong to leave out important detail that some readers need. So if extra detail is essential for some, consider using an appendix or appendices for this in paper reports, or attached electronically if sent by e-mail.

11 Always keep readers' cultural expectations and competence in business English in mind, and write accordingly.

12 Check what you have written for both sense and logic.

13 Check your writing for other mistakes too, including using a spell and grammar check in the variety of English you have used for your target audience.

14 Issue and check both the outcomes and the feedback after your audience has received your report or review.

Structure of reports

We don't want to be too prescriptive by suggesting you use a report template. As we've mentioned, formal reports are far less frequent than they used to be, and also may not be appropriate in a global context.

The tips we have just given you will definitely help you structure your reports and there is also a writing method called the inverted pyramid system that we'll explain now.

The inverted pyramid system

Journalists and news reporters are taught the concept of using the inverted pyramid to find out or decide which information is so important that it needs to go into their reports first. As shown in Figure 9.1, the pyramid is turned upside down, with its base at the top. That's where you write the most important points. Important supporting information

FIGURE 9.1 Using the inverted pyramid to write business reports

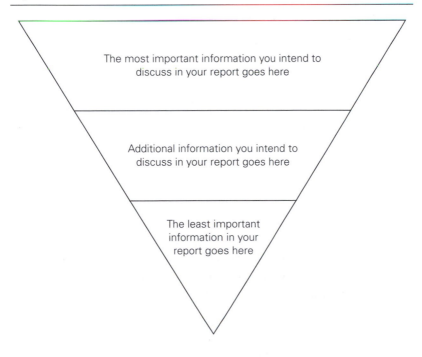

The most important information you intend to discuss in your report goes here

Additional information you intend to discuss in your report goes here

The least important information in your report goes here

follows in the next segment. Then, finally, you write the least important points at the tip of the pyramid.

Journalists then find these six very important questions help them work out the level of importance:

- Who is the event about?
- What is the event about?
- Where has the event occurred?
- When did the event occur?
- Why did the event happen?
- How did the event happen?

You may often be able to adapt this model for your reports, particularly when it comes to deciding which points are important and worth including. In a business context, not all the six questions will always be relevant. In view of this, we have rephrased and re-sequenced the questions to help you use them, for what could be an otherwise daunting task:

- What is the subject, topic or issue?
- Why is the subject, topic or issue important?
- Who is the subject, topic or issue about?
- When did the subject, topic or issue arise, or when could it arise?
- Where is the subject, topic or issue happening?
- How can the subject, topic or issue be made **comprehensible** and, therefore, dealt with suitably?

Activity

Try to get hold of a business report, preferably from the organization you work in, and analyse it to see if it follows the pyramid structure. Ask yourself the six questions as you go through it.

How has the report matched up? Which questions were relevant and which weren't? Have you thought of any questions that would help you more? List your observations here.

_____

_____

_____

_____

_____

_____

Different writing styles for different reports

If you are required to write an audit report, for example, you will need to write objective communication that's fair, impartial and unbiased, and results from a balanced assessment of all relevant facts and circumstances. You might think you won't have to develop the creative writing style that a marketing executive might consider a must. By now, you'll be seeing that we don't necessarily agree. Even the most objective business writers can go the step further: to make themselves individuals who *shine* through the way they write and whose readers are grateful for the 'signposts' they provide.

So, if you have to make recommendations in a report, highlight these. Prioritize key messages and any milestones, enable – and, if this is not exceeding your brief, *persuade* – readers to take the right action.

Some simple examples of helpful expressions are:

- This review shows how we can reduce expenditure by $10,000 this year without reducing customer service.
- In particular, these shortcomings mean we cannot launch the project as planned.
- Most importantly, your decision is needed on item 3.
- We need to ask the HR Department to increase the staffing arrangements for this quarter.
- These figures comfortably exceed the target for the year.

We've examined in earlier chapters how people from most cultures appreciate the personal touch, to some degree or other. Whether your culture is reserved or expressive, the expression of human interest shown in these short extracts can be very well received. Another example could be ending a report where company results have been good, with something on the lines of: Congratulations to the team.

Activity

Do you have to write reports? Even if you don't, you probably have to read them from time to time. What features make it easier for you to read a report? What features make reading more difficult, or less appealing, in any way? Is it layout? Does pyramid structuring help? Is it vocabulary? Is it tone – or something else? Jot down your findings here, as it's likely to help you write reports in the future.

_____

_____

_____

_____

_____

_____

Our feeling is that reports need never appear 'inhuman' or boring. If you are enthusiastic about what you write, it shows (as we discussed in Chapter 7). Enthusiastic business writers can have the power to make almost any reader interested in their reports – be the subject shipping law, gas safety, underwater cables, automotive parts, insurance, engineering plants, transportation, medical equipment... to name just a few!

Making your mark and anticipating questions

Can you see patterns in effective business writing emerging throughout the book? In Chapter 4 we highlighted the importance of anticipating likely questions when you deliver a presentation. The same advice applies when you write reports otherwise people can feel that you are wasting their time – even if their culture prevents them from saying this to your face.

Anticipating questions – and asking questions yourself – is a particularly valuable approach when you write reports containing points that you know may be complex, or likely to lead to vigorous debate. Cover those points and you will be noticed by key people for all the right reasons, including:

- for being systematic;
- for thinking around the subject;
- for making their life easier.

There can be compelling reasons to stop and consider before you hit the 'send' button to e-mail a report to your boss. The advice we're now going to give is particularly relevant if you are new to report writing or find yourself having to write reports for a multicultural organization.

Something we're noticing in this respect is that some cultures haven't in the past had to write formalized reports, but now find they must. We'll be discussing in Chapter 10 how some Asian cultures, as just one example, may traditionally have focused more on face-to-face meetings than on written communication generally, which naturally includes reports.

So the tips we offer now should be particularly helpful, not just in saving time and money, but also in strengthening the effectiveness of cross-cultural business interaction. This case study demonstrates what we mean.

CASE STUDY

A boss asked a member of his multicultural team to write up a monthly report, on the progress of an engineering project.

The person involved sent an e-mail, headed 'Progress Report'. He started by writing: 'I did this...' and then simply itemized bullet points that listed his actions.

The boss had to send an e-mail by return: 'So, *why* did you do those things?'

The member of staff wrote back 'I did them because...' and set out the reasons.

The boss then sent another e-mail: 'So, what were the *outcomes*?'

Can you see how this was ineffective 'report writing' by the member of staff? Wasn't it unnecessary and expensive duplication of work for the boss to have to send follow-up e-mails, just to get the information he needed right from the outset? Can you see that the boss may also have been irritated by this inefficiency on the report writer's part?

As you can see from this case study, which is also shown as a decision tree in Figure 9.2, the request from the boss seems simple enough – but a little more consideration on the writer's part could really have paid dividends.

The easy option for the report writer is to hit the send button and cut out the 'or' phase shown in the figure. We suggest this would be wrong. The writer would do better to ask himself or herself what the boss's request really means. If this isn't done, then there's much iteration, wasting of time and effort and, importantly, real damage to the perception of 'brand you'. It's simply not **smart**.

Activity

Consider the types of report you may be asked to write at work. For each, list the kind of things you should think about before writing – for example, what am I really being asked to do? What questions may I be asked? Keeping a checklist of areas to cover for the various writing assignments will help you – and it should soon become a natural habit.

_____

_____

_____

_____

_____

_____

FIGURE 9.2   Decision tree relating to a monthly report

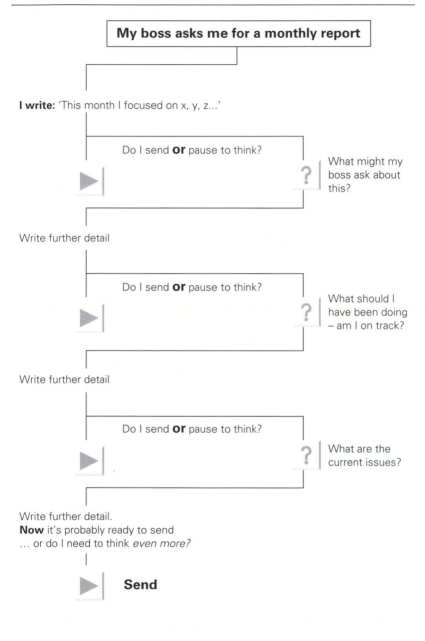

Writing can put up unintended barriers

Let's touch again on the use of the passive voice in writing, also mentioned in Chapter 8. The active voice is where the subject does the action. Sentences that show this are:

> The IT Department is currently reviewing this issue.
> The Treasurer highlighted the problems involved.

The passive voice is where the subject of the active clause becomes secondary; where it is acted upon or receives the action. Often the word 'by' is added, as you see in the following sentences:

> The issue is currently being reviewed by the IT Department.
> The problems involved are highlighted by the Treasurer.

In both these examples, we can still see who is doing the action. But sometimes the passive is used in reports without any reference to ownership – and then it can become problematic for readers to understand who does what (if anything). An example of a passive that can lead to uncertain outcomes is: 'This issue is currently being reviewed.' A reader may be uncertain about who is carrying out the review. The context may indicate this, but often it does not. In any event, why make your reader have to refer too closely to context, when your meaning can be crystal clear if you write the active form?

The structure you design always matters, even in a report that essentially only describes facts. Every word should add value so that readers know, almost at a glance:

- what the situation was or is;
- who is responsible for getting it right;
- who does what next and when.

Technical reports in a global context

In a global context, many reports written by non-native English speakers will be at a technical level and the standard of written English can vary enormously. It's all the more reason to have someone act as that important editor to check the finished product, as we mentioned earlier. But there's an additional point to make here too. This is that much of the writing will relate to technical issues for which there is a common understanding, regardless of language: namely 'how things work'. This can often be expressed in non-verbal language, such as drawings, mathematics, and so on.

Often a diagram can replace an enormous amount of written text, so it can be a very good idea in a multicultural context. It's also eco-friendly, saving paper where people are still using it. So, there are times when a picture can speak volumes, and work better than words on their own. Using basic shapes to compile flow charts works wonders in explaining complex processes, as do graphs when it comes to scrutinizing figures and trends – which can otherwise get a lot of readers scratching their heads. Similarly, if you use illustrations that are simple in design and very **clear**, (with a brief caption or description below) you can save readers time, and appeal to different learning modes.

Executive summaries

The content of every report matters. In addition, the considered opinion you're likely to provide should be welcome and valuable to readers – but this will only happen if it's readily recognized. Your readers are likely to be pressed for time, so you may find an executive summary a particularly useful tool. It's a summary of what the busy executive who needs to read it, needs to see. The reader often wants to see the key messages and core data: that is, the very heart of the report, instantly.

The summary can appear at the beginning or end and usually contains the key findings of the report. If you imagine that this chapter about structure is a report, we could end it, as we are doing now, by summarizing its key findings as follows:

- Identify your organization's stance on reports in general.
- If collaborating, make sure someone takes responsibility for editing the final document into a cohesive whole, with a consistent style and tone.

- If you don't actively highlight key messages and findings in your reports, don't assume that readers can identify them.

- Make reports logical and seamless, to have the right impact (so don't rely on cutting and pasting Word documents).

- Include a clear summary where you can.

- Write concisely and construct reports with the busy executive in mind.

Worksheet

Section A: Knowing your theory

Based on what you have understood from this chapter, respond to the following questions and statements by ticking the 'Yes' or 'No' boxes.

		Yes	No
1	Do reports need to be written in isolation, without considering the target audience?	☐	☐
2	Do all reports have a common purpose?	☐	☐
3	The inverted pyramid involves asking the six questions: Who...? What...? Where...? When...? Why...? How...?	☐	☐
4	Highlighting recommendations in your report helps get messages across.	☐	☐
5	Your reports are likely to be dull if you're not enthusiastic about your business.	☐	☐
6	Do you need to anticipate questions readers may ask, particularly when your report covers complex or debatable issues?	☐	☐
7	Should you use the active voice if you want to bring life to your report?	☐	☐
8	Executive summaries serve no purpose as an overview for readers who are pressed for time.	☐	☐

Section B: Reporting duty calls!

You can take a guess on what sort of exercise we ask you to try out here! Using the bullets and checklist in the chapter, write a report based on what you think is an issue or topic of concern, maybe even something to be raised with your management team. Don't forget to include diagrams, charts or graphs where you think words alone will not make the impression you want.

Alternatively, you could analyse a report that you know could be improved. Apply the pyramid approach to increase its impact and clarity.

You may even want to send the report to your manager when you have finished writing it. This will show that you are more **confident** in believing in 'brand you' and feedback will help you to become more **clear**, should this be needed.

Happy reporting!

Chapter Ten
Writing agendas, notes and minutes of meetings

Managers can be so wrong in assuming global teams speak the same language. And where there are misunderstandings, there are mistakes.

The effect of the digital age on meetings

The world over, a large proportion of people's working week is spent in meetings. They are certainly meant to be a valuable management tool, but are you totally convinced that every business meeting you've attended recently has yielded a 'return on investment'?

In the West, it's long been a business mantra that time is money. So maybe meetings should come with a price label attached and be subject to a cost-benefit analysis! Financial recession, among other factors, has made many organizations realize that communicating electronically in virtual meetings via teleconferences, websites, forums and e-mail can, when handled well, be as effective and certainly cost less than physical meetings.

Naturally, there are cultural, and office subcultural issues, as to why meeting in person can still be the preferred option. That said, we're beginning to notice an interesting development in countries where the traditional cultural expectation was that people always needed face-to-face meetings to do business.

Let's take China as one example. Many Chinese business people tell us that even a few years ago, the concept of time as money didn't resonate with them, as it does now. A booming market economy brings a new sense of immediacy. Handbooks on how to do business in China previously (and understandably) stressed the importance of developing relationships through hosting and attending meetings. Written business paperwork was not traditionally seen as something Chinese managers were expected to do. This still holds true in many cases, but today we see a perceptible shift away from meetings as the norm, towards more *written* business communication.

As Chinese businesses become inundated with burgeoning enquiries, orders and ever-opening global opportunities, their staff are writing more and more than ever before. The electronic age can clearly help them keep abreast of the ensuing workload more quickly and more economically than holding meetings as a matter of course. The two methods are increasingly going side by side.

Were we at the same meeting?

Have you been ever been at a business meeting with colleagues or stakeholders and each of you had a quite different recollection of what the outcomes were? You may even have been known to ask 'Were we at the same meeting?' If so, you certainly won't be alone!

This can happen when the meeting is in your own language. So it's easy to imagine how much more complicated – even stressful – meetings can be when they're held in English and it's not your native language.

Even people's approach to the meetings cycle can be culture-based. Let's take a look at Europe this time. Some Europeans believe that, if a meeting is justified, then there should be a pre-meeting to plan the meeting, possibly sub-meetings about main meetings, not to forget post-meetings! But others think the opposite. They believe meetings only work if those attending have the power to make decisions then and there. With such differences in communication approach, it's all about managing target audience's expectations.

Added to this, although English may appear to be the language of common currency in a meeting, it will be used in different ways by different speakers. This is another reason why it's best to deal with this issue at the outset – before problems arise when it gets to recording decisions in written form at the end of the meeting. It can be really worthwhile to have a short introductory session at the start. This gives an opportunity to check attendees' shared understanding of:

- the meeting's purpose;
- the terminology used;
- whether decisions are needed and can be made at the time.

As we've already mentioned, instantaneous decision making may be alien to some (for example hierarchical) cultures. They expect to have to group consensus outside the meeting, before any decision is binding.

The introduction also gives an opportunity to give out a list of specific vocabulary, or glossary of terms: words necessary for all to understand, for the meeting to run smoothly. If it's a technical meeting, for example, you may be surprised how even technical terms and jargon can be used to mean different things, as we discussed in Chapter 9. If it's a financial meeting, then even the way numbers or dates are expressed can vary from country to country, as you will see in Chapter 14. That's why it's helpful to explain the convention you use.

If you then ask if anyone needs clarification or any other assistance, it further helps create a more relaxed atmosphere. That's going to be good for everyone, isn't it?

What will go on your agenda?

An agenda simply means a list of things to be done or considered. It assists the smooth running of a meeting.

If it's your job to write an agenda, here are some guidelines to help:

- Write an agenda that's specific to the meeting and focuses on results.

- Prepare people for why the meeting is necessary.

- Have you alerted contributors to prepare materials for circulation? If so, have you given them a deadline? Have you checked they will observe it? Could you do any more to help?

- Set the best order possible for items to appear.

- Make sure topics are clearly defined and well set out, taking house style into account.

- Do attendees have to read anything before the meeting? If so, do you suggest this, even enable them to do this, perhaps by means of a relevant hyperlink?

- Circulate the agenda well in advance of the meeting.

Ideally, agree the agenda with any chairperson involved, as far in advance of the meeting as possible. Then give people notice of the agenda, otherwise how can they be fully prepared? In an ideal world, you e-mail papers (or less often these days, send them by post), usually a minimum of two or three working days before the meeting. So, optimally, you need to have all information available well before this.

The agenda needs to take into account likely objectives, such as discussing and taking key strategic decisions; reviewing operations; communicating with others to inform or get input; considering and enabling successful succession planning throughout the organization; and ensuring that the company follows the right procedures, for example for compliance.

Can you see why planning and writing a good agenda presents your opportunity to be **sophisticated**, **clear** and **confident** and help manage a meeting's success before it even starts? It's disappointing – and it's hugely inefficient – if meetings go ahead without clarity or agreement about who contributes, or what information they need to have. If the starting point is wrong, then the meeting's not on track to succeed from the outset, is it?

Activity

Do you have a convention on how to conduct important meetings in your organization? If so, does it meet the preparation guidelines we suggest? If not, or if you think it should be reviewed, try listing the elements that could be improved in your business environment.

_____

_____

_____

_____

_____

_____

Action sheets

Action sheets are an essential part of the storyline of your meeting's minutes. But you can't write action sheets until you have accurately recorded what's happened. When it comes to multicultural meetings, this can be easier said than done. So we would like to give you some tips to develop your skills in this connection. During the meeting:

- Stay calm and **confident**.

- Concentrate on the meaning of what is being said, rather than focusing on every word (a common pitfall in multicultural meetings).

- Resist personal interpretation.

- Ask questions to clarify things, to ensure that you get the whole picture (before the meeting moves on).

- Question what technical terms mean, if you are not sure.

- Check as far as you can (either personally or via the chairperson) that speakers understand the remit of the meeting – and that any problems that need to be solved, are being solved.

Don't be the person who is puzzled – or left without the answers – when it comes to writing the minutes and recording the follow-up after the meeting. If, as the person taking the minutes, you can do your best to be seen as a co-manager of the meeting, do so. Be **sophisticated**, and **confident** enough to ask when you are unsure of what is being said, or where a particular point is leading.

In most organizations, meetings and minutes are usually action-oriented. Yet, even when writing in their native language, both native English and non-native English people taking minutes can feel their work is complete if they record an outline sketch of each action. What's more, this can be within the main minute and is often in passive form.

Do you remember what the passive mood in English is? This sentence will remind you: 'It was decided that a report should be submitted to the next meeting.'

This writing isn't ideal. Simply recording actions isn't the end of the story, is it? The writer has hidden the action required in the passive sentence. We don't actually know who is to submit the report.

Ditch the passives – and substitute the actives and the 'concretes', for example: 'The finance director needs to report on action 123 at the next meeting on 5 November.'

Once you are clear what the actions are, it's a real help to all concerned to record these in a column on the right-hand side of the minutes, or write them on a separate page, for subsequent circulation. In addition, an ongoing summary table of open actions (from previous meetings) and new actions is particularly helpful. It's also useful for the chairperson, who can then easily review and follow up actions that are outstanding. In this way, your **smart** minutes and action log both become an *effective management tool*.

Don't forget our advice on house style in Chapter 2. People don't always realize that minutes are corporate written communication too and we often find various departments within the same organization write minutes differently, for no good reason.

Activity

Taking the ideas we suggest, why not design a layout for your meeting notes and a rolling action log in the space below? You may need to revise any existing standard you have, or create a new one. This will help you write effectively – both from your and your readers' points of view.

_____

_____

_____

_____

_____

_____

Style tips for minutes

If we look on minutes as a business story, we can shed the wrong image that so many people have, which is that minutes are a boring, 'dead' record of something that took place at some point in time. Maybe you can even make your mark here, as minutes are a form of writing likely to have an impact not just on the present, but on the future too. They are vital – so use word power skills and write them with vitality.

If, let's say, you are recording discussions, try avoiding writing the same word (such as 'said') over and over. Consider the many easy alternatives that exist in English, such as: 'stated, discussed, proposed, reported, considered', and so on. If something is 'decided' you could also use alternatives such as: 'confirmed, approved, verified, resolved', and so on. A meeting can have 'ended' and it could also have 'concluded' or 'finished'. Using alternatives is one way of energizing your writing and it's still plain English that people understand.

By turning on your **clear**, **comprehensible** and **smart** buttons once again, you can write minutes that keep readers focused on the task in hand.

Defining timescales will help

Many organizations have a rule that minutes must be written and circulated within 48 hours. Does your organization have any guidelines on this? Even if it seems overly challenging at the time, it can be in everyone's interests to write up minutes as soon as possible. Why? Because the sooner we record discussions and decisions taken, the better our recall is.

We've all found our 'best outline meeting notes in the world' can make less sense when we put them to one side for a while. Attention strays easily in the digital age. In a world where newer events and more recent discussions compete for our attention, we have to be careful not to be distracted from following through.

Other people's memories will fade as well. If you need their agreement or if they require amendments (and this is all part of the minute-writing cycle), it's easier to get this finalized sooner rather than later.

Converting notes to minutes – the vital stages

Use a good layout to impress your readers before they go on to read the subject matter. Judge how much they know of the topics in question – and how much they need to see in the minutes. Include references made to important specifics, such as:

- events, dates, locations;
- money, budgets;
- contracts;
- names of departments, people, outside bodies etc.

Use informative headings and paragraphs. If you use headings for new subjects and paragraphs for each new point made, people first know which items are of most relevance to them. This is the vital 'what's in it for me?' factor. You then enable them to read the minutes in short sections. Remember that not everyone who reads minutes has to read every item.

For example: 'Successful launch of Geronimo Project – 2013' will make more impact and be easier for a reader to find than 'Project launch'. If your busy manager just needs to check the status on that project he or she will thank you for highlighting it – and for the figurative 'pat on the back' you have expressed in writing that word '*successful*'.

Write as positively as possible. As you know by now, this entire book is about you identifying personal and organizational values you need readers to see, so show these. If targets have been reached that's great news, so why not use a heading that highlights this? If there is any shortfall in performance this will have to be recorded. But there are always reasons for shortfalls – and there are usually solutions. Highlight these in your minutes where you can.

Review of minutes

Review your minutes (and maybe you'll need to ask your manager or chairperson to review them as well, depending on your organizational culture) before you issue them. Check they are correct on every level, as we highlighted in the global word power skills guide in Chapter 8. We will be giving specific pointers on how to proofread and check the quality of your writing generally in Chapter 13.

We're aware that in multicultural teams minutes are sometimes wrongly 'corrected' when reviewed either by the minute-writers' native or non-native English managers or other colleagues. Has this ever happened to you? It can seem a shame if your business English is more accurate than, for example, your manager's. But sometimes we all have to accept we need to write to suit our team leader's or line manager's preferences. After all, that person will be (or should be) taking overall responsibility for every piece of writing that goes out. And minutes are hugely important documentation. But if you keep your writing clear, unambiguous and a true record of what happened, you enhance your chances of success.

So, draw on all the tips we have given you in this chapter to shine throughout these vital stages. Your minutes aren't necessarily about finishing the meeting process: on the contrary, in business they're more often about creating an ongoing dialogue and a continuing story.

Your skill is to ensure that what you write helps every player in that storyline:

- to understand why there was a meeting of which the minutes were a record;
- to understand their role – and what they and their fellow players need to do next, why and when by.

Worksheet

Section A: Knowing your theory

Based on what you have understood from this chapter, answer the following questions by ticking the 'Yes' or 'No' boxes.

	Yes	No
1 Thanks to digital technologies, is there a perceptible shift towards more written business communications?	☐	☐
2 In multicultural meetings, can it be useful to have a short glossary of specific terms used?	☐	☐
3 Do you agree that producing sketchy notes is fine, because everyone remembers the detail of the discussion?	☐	☐
4 Is it all right if agendas are unstructured?	☐	☐
5 Is writing minutes purely about recording decisions?	☐	☐
6 When taking minutes, do you need to come across as **confident** and **sophisticated**, especially when it comes to asking when you are unsure of what is being said, or where a particular point is leading?	☐	☐
7 If your minutes and action log are **smart** enough, can they become an effective management tool?	☐	☐
8 Does using well-designed and informative headings for subjects enable people to see which agenda items and minutes are of most relevance to them?	☐	☐

Section B: What's your agenda?

In this chapter, we have given you helpful tips to use when writing agenda, notes and minutes of business meetings. For this exercise, we would like you to:

1 Get hold of a copy of the minutes of a business meeting that you wrote, maybe some time ago – or the minutes that somebody else has written (regarding a meeting that you know something about).

2 Match tips from this chapter alongside the minutes. See if there are any gaps, or aspects of the minutes that you now think could be improved.

3 Rewrite what you have highlighted, using the tips you have chosen.

Chapter Eleven
Personal and company promotion in the digital age

Let people see who you are through your writing.
And while you're at it, be the best you can!

Traditional public relations (PR) promotion and PR promotion in the digital age

In Chapter 3 we discussed the importance of identifying 'brand you' alongside your organizational brand, and knowing which voice to use in your business communication each time you write. Do remember this now, as we look at 'traditional forms' of PR and website promotion, and draw your attention to the unstoppable rise in promotion via social media, explored further in Chapter 12.

Understanding the goal you need to achieve by getting information about you into the news is what all PR is about. For example, financial PR is largely about managing the reputation of a stock-listed company in the financial press and managing relationships with investors. Product PR gets messages about a product into the media with the aim of increasing sales in the long term. Brand PR is about creating or building a brand and a certain image (whether personal or company) in the media, and so on.

Personal promotion today

Just a few years ago, personal promotion was largely considered to be what you did when searching for a job. People sent paper covering letters and CVs (also called *resumés* in the United States, France and elsewhere and '*biodata*' in the East).

Nowadays, online sites dominate job searching, for example general job sites such as monster.com (global), reed.co.uk (UK), or naukri.com (India). There are also vast numbers of recruitment agencies' websites offering details of vacancies at the click of a button.

Increasingly, LinkedIn and other social media sites garner much of the market by advertising jobs to targeted professionals. It's true that a well-written CV remains paramount: but personal promotion in the digital age is much more than a CV. It needs extra flourishes such as social media links to a personal website, blog or webzine. For this reason we deal with writing CVs in Chapter 12.

In general terms, self-promotion means being **confident**, seizing the advantage to enhance your personal visibility and your professional (even in a sense 'street') credibility. Be **smart** and **sophisticated**: realize the opportunity this form of business writing offers in getting you noticed and remembered for the right reasons.

Activity

Do you remember we asked you to jot down words that best captured your professional qualities and 'brand you' in Chapter 3? In Chapter 7, we asked you to jot down power words relevant to what you do. Revisit these words and now write down which ones it may be useful to include when you next write (or update) your CV. Are there other words to add?

_____

_____

_____

_____

_____

Are you creating the right publicity?

Once you decide you need to arrange publicity, make sure it's the right publicity. There are a number of ways to achieve this – either online (including via free or paid PR distribution sites) or offline. You can pay external advertising agencies to promote your products or services, or write your own copy that is interesting and has impact. Here are some ways to achieve the right publicity:

- Write a press release (that highlights you, your staff, your cause/ charity, product/service, etc) that's in some way newsworthy. Highlight why your event/product/service launch is worth putting in the news. For example, have you received a major donation, won a major contract or award/made some groundbreaking innovation?

- Use your website and links to others' websites.

- Contribute articles to or advertising via social networking sites.

- Use your expert professional knowledge to write an article for publication.

- Write a contribution to a topical, professional debate featured in a newspaper, magazine, television, radio or relevant website, webzine, blog, etc.

- Write a free tips column on your specialist subject in a newspaper, magazine, website, blog or webzine (on a one-off or regular basis).

- Offer your advice or expertise on social networking media sites (for example Facebook, Twitter, LinkedIn).

- Contact your local newspaper or a specialist magazine or journal to see if an advertorial can feature your copy. (An advertorial is a feature article that also promotes your product or service in clear terms. It often appears labelled as 'Promotion' or 'Advertorial' on the top of the pages.)

- When you write, use the basic journalistic principle of answering the six vital questions: Who...? What...? Where...? Why...? When...? How...?

- Use the inverted pyramid system we showed in Chapter 9 to structure your writing.

If you are published, the fact an editor has chosen you (probably over others) gives you a great endorsement as a professional, sometimes at no financial cost! Readers are often sceptical about claims made in paid advertisements. They're more likely to see editorial coverage as objective and often react more positively.

Editors are generally passionate about their publications or websites. Vast numbers of unsolicited press releases come through each week, so they only choose the best. They are likely to choose:

- those of most general interest to their readers (given the sector);
- those of most specific interest to their readers (for example in terms of news topicality, ongoing debate);
- the best written – those that can be published as they are (without the need to correct or edit, space permitting).

In your home country you'll have an idea of which publications to target. If you're looking for new global markets, research appropriate publications and influential websites. Gather local knowledge: ask around or engage professional PR services. Stay accountable, ensure that your writing:

- conveys your message correctly;
- is fit for purpose;
- is published at the right time (which is especially important when you're promoting something);
- contains some call to action or some way to create a dialogue;
- includes your name and all relevant contact details.

Standard layout of a press release

A standard way of laying out a press release is as follows.

First, insert the release date.

Use word power to insert an interesting, attention-grabbing title.

Insert your personal and organization contact details, so the editor knows who to contact for more information. Mark the article 'For editor's attention' – preferably with the person's name as well. For the main content:

- Type the document using double spacing and ensure that it's immaculately presented and contains no mistakes.

- The headline and first paragraph should contain key information, such as mentioning the point of the release.

- Avoid jargon; highlight benefits to a wider audience, where possible.

- Explain the importance of the press release.

- Make it relevant to the publication, readership and area in question; use vocabulary that's right for the audience.

- If possible, give a short, enthusiastic, interesting quote from a named spokesperson: 'people buy people'.

- Also put personal or your organization contact details at the end of your release, for readers to contact a named person (and make sure you tell that person, if it is someone else).

Doing the extra to make it work

Editors reserve the right to edit your copy: they use space available to their best advantage, not yours. That's why building a relationship is well worth the investment. Try to mark things for a named person's attention and telephone that person if you can, so you literally have a voice! Finally, try to ensure that your contact details appear in any published article, so you become an accessible person and your story can take you into readers' futures.

Here's an extract from a press release for an Indian audience that introduces a splash of local Indian English.

CASE STUDY   Pearl Crown Hotels: Indian PR extract

Parikshit Mehra has been appointed as the new CEO of Pearl Crown Hotels, a premier hotel chain in South-East Asia, and is taking over the management of the hotels from Shivam Gowain, who is now retiring from service.

Says Mr Mehra, 'I am delighted and highly honoured to work for Pearl Crown; I have always admired the way this hotel chain respects its customers and staff attentively and I will prioritize this from the beginning of my tenure.'

Pearl Crown Hotels, which is currently ranking as number 5 in the top 20 international hotels in India, is prized for its customer satisfaction in the Subcontinent.

Can you see there are some style differences over standard English, for example 'Says Mr Mehra' rather than 'Mr Mehra says'? And the sentiment is very appealing: Mr Mehra is not only delighted but also 'highly honoured' to work for Pearl Crown. The words emphasize respect and customer service; much of the vocabulary is quite formal and long sentences, separated with semi-colons, are used. Aside from these characteristics though, much of the English used is global, as the press release also targets readers worldwide.

Put yourself on the map for the right reasons: write to reflect differing cultural sensibilities, depending on the country or region you do business with. Just as with letters and e-mails, you could begin and end with a customary salutation or greeting. Then consider including cultural or historical background relevant to your market. Anything that strikes a chord, and makes your readers sit up, take interest and then invest in the product or service your PR is promoting, makes sound commercial sense.

Even within a single country, the publications you target may use very different writing styles. At one end of the spectrum in the UK, certain British tabloids use very informal, sensational headlines, often based on colloquial puns. Others remain far more formal. Be aware of similar variations in your target markets.

Do you ever have to write press releases at work? If so, have they ever been for an overseas market? In which case, have you considered when to use global or glocal English?

Activity

Even if you don't write press releases, look out for random examples in the world at large. How do different organizations from different countries write global press releases in English? Compare and contrast styles to see what works best in your opinion, and why. Write your findings here.

_____

_____

_____

_____

_____

_____

Words to make an impact

In any press release, your headline sets the scene. This tip applies to website headlines too, so bear it in mind in the website section that follows. Just contrast these two headlines:

Spectacular year for ABC
Very good year for ABC

The first grabs readers' attention and interest much more, through use of a dynamic word '*spectacular*' and the use of bold text. This pattern is repeated in the next two examples.

Contract delight for ABC workers
Contract won by ABC

The first example introduces an added element over the second: the human element. It's a good move, given that 'the people factor' is something on which every organization's success largely depends. So use the tips given in Chapter 7: make the right impact.

Evaluate every word you choose as you have the power to choose the right words! For example, check whether you really want to describe every award you win as 'prestigious'. It's a great word by itself, but if four press releases in the same publication use it, it becomes devalued, losing impact.

Activity

What attention-grabbing words can you think of for writing titles for press releases for your organization? List them here.

_____

_____

_____

_____

_____

_____

And if you have to place any notice or advertisement in a publication, or write anything that's time-specific, ensure that readers see it at the right time, or it may be useless.

Writing for websites

Websites used to be the first port of call in a company's online promotional presence. In the digital age they are often the secondary one: the one people turn to once you've got them interested via your social media activities, for example. That said, they are supremely important, being able to offer fuller details than the other online pro-motional media.

User-friendly content

The trouble is that visitors sometimes only take four seconds before exiting a site they don't like, even though the site initially met their search criteria. Write so they like what they see and stay longer.

It's not for this book to show you how to set up a website, its navigation or make it earn advertising revenue. There are specialists and lots of information out there to help you. But we can give you helpful tips on how to write user-friendly content effectively:

- Your website is your shop window, so to speak. Dress it attractively, using tips we gave you in Chapter 4. Use the right fonts, the right size of type, etc.

- All the activities you have carried out so far in this book have given you a heightened awareness of your corporate identity, as well as 'brand you'. Show this in the words you use.

- Maintain quality and professionalism by ensuring that there are no mistakes in what you write.

- Remember, your website may be viewed by people all over the world. Judge to what extent you need to use global versus glocal English. You will by now understand you have to write for different cultural sensibilities and we'll be giving you more examples shortly. Remember, it isn't just about generating clicks: you want users to become loyal readers or customers.

- Understand that you have to set out your wares, attractively packaged in great writing. Accurately describe what you offer, engage readers and keep them glued if possible. You want to sell, don't you?

- You can do this by writing content that sees things from readers' perspectives as well as your own. For example, can you write about problems you know your readers are likely to encounter, and for which you have the solution? Outline this. Frequently asked questions (FAQs) can also be a good idea.

- Write your home page (called the landing page in some countries) as the focus of your website, which users start from and can come back to when restarting their browsing.

- Write hyperlinks throughout to take visitors to further relevant information and topical discussions about the product or service in question.

- Understand the relevance of keywords: the words and phrases people use when they do an online search for a product or service.

We mentioned in Chapter 4 how people get tired reading large amounts of text, especially on computer, tablet devices or smartphone screens. We discussed how good web writers break copy into sections, often subdividing these further with bold headings and links.

Web designers know the importance of structuring websites and provide site maps for navigation. These maps help writers to structure and signpost their content too. Write your separate sections with good, attention-grabbing headings, outlining the 'what's in it for me?' or 'aha! I get it' factor to readers. Use what's known as anchorage, a journalistic term referring to the use of headlines and images that hook people into reading the article, newspaper or magazine (and therefore buying it). Break down your content into easily digestible, focused sections that link with your network of interconnected pages, accessed via tabs, menus or hyperlinks.

Writing global versus glocal English on websites

If you have a local business, how can you adapt to take your business global? Conversely, if you work for a global business, how can you bring out local aspects, to show you care about the culture of your customer base?

Adidas, a global sportswear brand, offers an example. With franchises dotted around the world, it has websites for each country where its products are most sold. Where possible, it uses both glocal English and the native language of the country but keeps its global website in global English.

Can you see the differences between global and glocal English in these examples?

CASE STUDY Adidas

Go get better, share your skills, compare yourself with the best and challenge your friends.

SOURCE: **www.adidas.com** – Adidas Global, 2012.

Criticism and self-doubt can paralyze the most talented athletes. Only a rare breed converts the stones thrown at them into milestones...

SOURCE: **www.adidas.com/in** – Adidas India, 2012.

The text in the first example is crisp, concise and clear. The second (from Adidas India) uses more sophisticated and poetic vocabulary; this type of approach can work well for Arab and Asia-Pacific cultures too.

Kentucky Fried Chicken (KFC) is another global player that knows how crucial it is to use global or glocal English in its websites. If you visit **http://www.kfc.com** you will see that the content uses global English, all about 'serving the world's best chicken'. But if you visit **http://www.kfc-arabia.com** you'll see glocal culture-relevant English too:

CASE STUDY KFC Arabia

All imported products are certified Halal by the Islamic authorities in the source country in order to meet and comply with the legislation of the Islamic countries where only Halal products are permitted for import.

Writing promotional content via social media to attract clients worldwide

We discuss social media in the next chapter, as it's the phenomenal driver of personal and company promotion today. Here we just touch on the way one player, LinkedIn, is used to promote businesses the world over with much success. It provides 'Groups' tabs for 'Discussions' of work-related issues and 'Promotions'. People use the latter to inform members of latest updates on their business products or services. This tip applies across the board: because new members to any platform may not know about your business, you always have to write your posts keeping them in mind too.

Advertising and promotional literature for a global market

Advertising is a challenging topic for any business working across borders. Points of interest to a local market may be of little relevance to a worldwide audience. For some cultures, who believe in developing relationships built and sustained over the years, it could be helpful to know that a company has 60 years of trading success. For others, for whom 'latest' means 'most up to date' this 60-year-old company may conjure up the vision of a commercial dinosaur. If you want to succeed, there are no short cuts in getting to understand the needs of your target audience and cutting the cloth of your advertising to suit, so to speak.

Here's a case study to show how one major global player approached the issue in one of its campaigns.

CASE STUDY HSBC

HSBC has around 7,500 offices around the world in 87 countries and territories. It's proud of its slogan 'the world's local bank' because it knows their service culture and offerings will need to vary, not just to regional but also to personal preference. As the company puts it: 'the more you look at the world, the more you recognise how people value things differently.'

Over the years, HSBC have run high profile advertising campaigns highlighting what they see as their unique selling point (USP) in grasping this concept. Some years back, they ran a picture campaign at airports across the world.

The campaign showed three photo images at a time, as pictures often speak volumes, with or without words.

One advertisement showed three mats. Each mat had a caption on it.
On the first, the caption was 'décor'.
On the second it was 'souvenir'.
On the third it was 'prayer mat'.

Another such advertisement showed three cars. Each car had a different caption beneath.

On the first it was 'freedom'.
On the second it was 'status symbol'.
And on the third it was 'polluter'.

The simplicity of expression in the HSBC campaign is very powerful, wouldn't you agree? It's deceptively easy: there will have been much hard work behind producing this. Most would agree the message is **clear** and **comprehensible**. Such simplicity is also elegant – and as we have suggested from our definition in Chapter 1, it's **sophisticated** too. How we see the mat or the car can be coloured by our cultural perspective – and also by our individual personality.

This chapter has shown you how to open your horizons as you write. It's not necessarily about directly translating brochures and other PR material as it stands. What's right for you personally – or for your company in your own market – may not work when trading internationally. Communicating digitally and potentially across borders requires different approaches.

Worksheet

Section A: Knowing your theory

Based on what you have understood from this chapter, respond to the following questions and statements by ticking the 'Yes' or 'No' boxes.

		Yes	No
1	PR is the same across all industries: it relates simply to product placement.	☐	☐
2	Is it true that promoting your professional profile online is increasingly important?	☐	☐
3	Using the inverted pyramid system can help when you write press releases.	☐	☐
4	Does one style of writing suit all publications?	☐	☐
5	Websites are the digital equivalent of a shop window.	☐	☐
6	If you trade globally, might you need to write website content that keeps different cultural sensibilities in mind?	☐	☐
7	Is 'the latest is best' a message that always works?	☐	☐
8	Communicating digitally and potentially across borders requires different approaches.	☐	☐

Section B: Promoting professionally

This chapter has focused on how best to exploit the power of print and digital media for publicity, especially when it comes to promoting yourself or your business, product or service.

Keeping the three Cs in mind (**clear**, **comprehensible** and **confident**), try the following exercises.

Has your company ever had a press release published in print? If so, consider how you might rewrite it now, to suit online social media networks (for example Facebook) better.

Take a good look at your organization's website. Are there areas where you think the content could be written differently? Is the necessary global–glocal balance there, for example? What changes would you make? Could you perhaps 'put yourself on the map' by suggesting these to anyone at work?

Chapter Twelve
Using word power skills with social networking media

In social media, the present changes to the past as we blink. But if our words make impact, they have the power to leap into the future.

www: words, words, words

www stands for the world wide web and the web is made up of words, words and more words. Whether we need to send an e-mail, register online, book tickets, access in-house software programs in banks, or carry out other transactions with businesses the world over, increasingly we need written words to use these convenient, life-changing, time-saving, cost-effective facilities.

This brings us to a phenomenal change in the way we can now communicate globally: social networking media. These media define web 2.0, the approach of sharing information and collaborating online and, for some, web 3.0 – where your own and the virtual reality start to merge, as in location-based applications (apps) such as foursquare. What all share in common is the facility to enable everyone to get in touch with anyone, anywhere, anytime. You can now find old friends and distant relatives through a quick search, and businesses can promote their products and services to an expansive target audience, which was previously limited to territorial borders.

Social networking media come via many platforms and, interestingly, fast-developing countries (such as India, Brazil and China) are among the front-runners in seizing the potential these platforms bring for the global promotion of corporate identities, up until now largely unknown outside their home markets. In so many ways, the platforms are becoming the major PR vehicles of the digital age.

Here's an outline of some current platforms:

- Facebook – at the time of writing, the world's largest two-way communication system with almost 1 billion users. There are about 60 billion clicks on 'likes' and written comments every month!

- Google+ – a virtual lounge for members to socialize with people, specifically or generally (for example classmates from universities, colleagues from a particular company, family members) via text, mobile and video chatting platforms.

- Twitter – the ultimate global talking shop with all sorts of dialogue, exchanges, debates, advertising, marketing and discussions, all within 'tweets' of 140 characters maximum.

- LinkedIn – a professional network where all matters related to business, careers, and employment are discussed and strictly professional connections are made.

- MySpace – a network that's now developed into a one-stop-shop for news, views, clips and comments on all things related to music, music videos and video games and on industry-related issues.

- Path – one of the newer sites that is currently taking off, that lets you see who looked at your post, photos or status update.

- Orkut – one of the first social media networks, devised by Google and now mainly used in Brazil and India.

- Plaxo – an online address book that synchronizes all contacts acquired via use of e-mail and social networking media sites.

- Weibo – a micro-blogging site in China. Written in Chinese, it's similar to Twitter and used by nearly half of China's 513 million net users or netizens in 2011.

- Hyves – the Dutch equivalent to Facebook, but where news and information on all things Dutch is also available.

The very nature of the media means these platforms are likely to change on an ongoing basis. The good news from this book's perspective is that the global word power skills writing system in Chapter 8 will help you write for new platforms too. The principles will largely remain the same, helping you adapt your writing for the marked shift in focus from product (as on websites and traditional promotional copy) to consumer. Being effective in the new media is less about selling, and more about your voice: at times personal, at times corporate.

It's about sharing information and experiences, sharing the latest multimedia developments, listening and reacting to what others are saying – and garnering people's interest. If people like the content, they are quite likely to become your 'brand advocates', telling their friends and contacts about what you sell or otherwise promote. You are likely to do this for them as well. It opens new dialogues, and consequently horizons, in this brave, new world into which we have been catapulted.

Interestingly, Twitter is the very site where we, the authors of this book (@wordpowerskills and @SudakshinaKina) first met. It started with polite tweets and exchanges. This led to us meeting up and swapping professional experiences about the changing face of global business communications thanks to new media technologies – which then brought about this book.

Now we'll focus on how to improve your business writing using the current top three social networking media sites in the list; Facebook, Twitter and LinkedIn.

Using a Facebook page to promote your product or service

Facebook has been a leader, going beyond the social remit to bring about professional interactions and communication. Individuals have their own accounts which come with their own *profiles* and there are *pages* for businesses. So, as Facebook members, we interact and stay updated with other members (or 'friends' – the generic term used here) via our *profiles*. Similarly, businesses can interact with and update members, who are customers or potential customers.

CASE STUDY BBC Entertainment television channel

A good case in point is BBC Entertainment, a British television channel that airs popular UK television programmes across the world.

The channel introduced a scheme asking viewers to review their programmes on their website, or comment on their Facebook page. Those who have written the best, most original comments, win BBC merchandise (for example DVDs and accessories).

This is not a random competition nor is it an offer. Those viewers who are fans of programmes would probably click 'Like' on the channel's Facebook page anyway. So, how long does it take them to write a comment on what they think of the channel and its programmes? Not long at all. Yet they now have an added incentive to visit the page regularly, to check on updates and results of who has been selected. And they continue to watch the programmes.

The scheme has worked well so far, and has been repeated for months, as we write. It's likely it will continue to do so, because it rakes in viewers and keeps them glued to the channel.

Business writing tips for Facebook pages and posts

The case study above is just one example of hundreds of businesses out there who now use a Facebook page to market their wares. Here are some suggestions on how to write your company page to help bring in more business.

First, ensure that essential details such as your brand logo (in the display picture box on the top-left side of the page), your web or postal addresses and a contact telephone number are distinctly available. This assures visitors that your page is genuine and not made by copycats.

Second, ensure that every post you write is engaging, and validly encourages users to click on the 'Like' hyperlink. Just as we write status updates on our personal Facebook profiles to get people to 'Like' and 'Comment' on them, use the same method when writing posts on your business pages. Ask yourself why should visitors read this post? For example:

CASE STUDY   Mocha Coffee

Good morning coffee-lovers!

> Had a hectic start to your day? Pop in to Mocha's for a nice warm brew (available in regular, medium and grand sizes) to keep you recharged! Click here to download a PDF of our wide-ranging menu: **www.mochacoffee.co.in/menu** (You will need to have Adobe Acrobat Reader installed on your device).

As you can see, the post is written in a friendly, engaging tone to attract customers (namely, Indian professionals who like this coffee chain, and Facebook). Yet all it talks about is its business: selling varieties of freshly brewed coffee to a café-going audience.

Third, each post should have that balance of interacting with visitors and promoting your business. Looking at this fictitious post as an example, do you think it works?

> Click here to see our new Autumn/Winter collection of shoes, bags, belts, etc:
> **www.amazingshoesandmore.com**.

We suggest two things are wrong here: a) the tone lacks enthusiasm and b) why should visitors click on the hyperlink? What's special about the new collection? What's meant by 'etc'? What other accessories does this site have on offer? All this information is missing but can be given with a few more words, for example:

Click here **www.amazingshoesandmore.com/autwint2013** to see our amazing new Autumn/Winter collection of leading designer shoes for him and her, gorgeous 'pick-me-up-now' bags, on-trend belts, smart ties and premium, hand-crafted cufflinks in silver and gold. Facebook customers will get a 30 per cent discount when purchasing online. Get your quote here: **www.amazingshoesandmore.com/offers**.

Also, note the use of adjectives here, for example 'leading,' 'gorgeous', 'smart' These are power words, right for the target market and describing the type of goods on sale. Adjectives such as 'designer', 'on-trend', 'hand-crafted' and 'premium' also work as keywords alongside the nouns, for example 'shoes' and 'cufflinks'.

Activity

You're about to launch an online business that sells a unique range of men's suits. Based on the examples we've shown, how would you write a post about this launch for your Facebook page? Remember to include keywords, and adjectives describing the quality of your goods to appeal to your target audience. Why should people buy from your website? What's special and exclusive about your business? What unique selling points (USPs) should appear? These pointers should help you write your ideas here.

_____

_____

_____

_____

_____

_____

Next, let's pause for thought. Just because users click on the 'Like' icon, does it necessarily mean they're going to buy whatever you are promoting on Facebook?

The answer is probably no, unless they have used or know your product or service and are pleased with their experience with it. Competitions and offers to win sample products aren't always effective. People see through them easily and they know that their chances of winning are very slim so they often don't bother to sign up. So, again, make your business writing engaging enough to make your customers eager to win the goods on offer. Here's an example.

Fancy a trip for two to the enchanting, luxurious beaches of Mauritius? Or a blissful yoga retreat in Coonoor, India? If you have been a Pay Monthly customer with us for the past 12 months, then visit our website and simply enter your name, e-mail address and the start date of your contract here: **www.mobiles4u.net/dec2011competition**.

This indicates to your target audience that the entrants for this competition have been narrowed down (so the odds of winning a trip increase). It also indicates that you appreciate your loyal customers.

Finally, remember that simply putting a page up on Facebook for the sake of it is not enough. Create relationships with users by interacting with them, showing that you exist and care – and are there to do business with them. If we want our messages to go viral, there may be a very strong case for using global rather than glocal English that may not be understood by all, as you will have seen by now. Also write to make your page lively and vibrant. Try interaction such as this:

- Reply to users' comments. This gives the added advantage that you have some right of reply and it can be useful for putting your viewpoint if any comments seem in any way negative.

- Ask fans or 'likers' for feedback on your product or service via questions in posts, or links to surveys.

- Share YouTube video clips about the latest media advertisements for your business.

- Offer informative insights or even funny anecdotes about events that go on within your organization (but be aware, in a global context, humour might not work for your target market's culture).

- Share good news, including favourable press coverage about your business.

It can pay great dividends to get it right. At the time of writing, the fast-food chain Subway is the number one most talked about brand on Facebook, outranking even Facebook itself. This shows how powerful the medium can be.

Activity

Do you view anybody else's company page on Facebook? Have you ever passed on a message to friends and, in a sense, become an unpaid advocate of someone's brand? If so, when and why was that? Can you analyse the language the brand in question used? What made the brand's message appealing? If it was in English, did the message use global or glocal English, with a local splash of colour? Jot your findings here; it may help you in the future.

_____

_____

_____

_____

_____

_____

To tweet or not to tweet? How to write for Twitter

Twitter is called the world's global talking shop because users (Twitterers or Tweeps etc) the world over do just that; they share their feelings, ideas, opinions, likes, disgust, complaints, suggestions and yes, even promote their businesses via posts, or tweets. The very name Twitter conjures up the tuneful little melodies of birdsong. Whether for personal or professional purposes, tweets should be short (obviously), sweet or sharp (depending on the context), **clear**, **comprehensible** (in terms of writing quality) and show that you are **confident** (yes, all the three Cs need to be covered here).

Twitter and other social media can have a language of their own

All social media bring new language and meanings. Facebook, for example, is introducing new terms such as 'defriend' or 'unfriend' (the opposite of 'friend') or giving a new meaning to 'Like' (that is, 'ticking the box' or 'registering we exist', which is not the same as 'like' in everyday language). Nor does 'top influencer' have the same meaning in LinkedIn say, as it does elsewhere, as we'll show later. Similarly, the use of hashtags in Twitter is also crossing over to mainstream. So we strongly advise you to check an online glossary of terms, as and when you start to use each of the media. We'll refer to some of the inevitable new jargon as we go.

Business writing tips for tweets

Once again, analyse what works and what doesn't, on a regular basis. For example, you will have noticed there's a quote at the beginning of each chapter in this book. Each is an original quote by @wordpowerskills that has been retweeted or 'favorited' (to use Twitter language) by followers from all over the world.

A pattern has emerged as to why tweeps chose the quotes they did. Each quote reflects the wordpowerskills brand: making the complex simple to understand. None involve direct selling but use accessible language to describe a generic business writing tip. Readers clearly chose tweets that meant something to them, either as inspiration or as a universal truth: 'Oh yes, that's true, we share a lot in common across the world!' Or because they knew the quote would help them at work – and they helpfully want to pass the message on.

Activity

Take time to read and think about the quotes starting each chapter to see which strike a chord with you, and why. Jot down your findings here.

_____

_____

_____

_____

_____

_____

Also take time to look at other random tweets and analyse what doesn't work. As an example, imagine you've just started following a new business consultancy and you receive a direct message (DM) from them: 'Welcome to our Twitter account. Now come on over and like us on Facebook.' If you then find they're not even following you back, how do you react to their DM? This real-life example can seem abrupt, even rude, although there's a pleasant enough greeting: 'Welcome'. Would you agree?

The problem, to our minds, is that the message is all about *them* and nothing to do with others. Being personable and professionally credible as part of *brand you* is as important on Twitter as everywhere else. There are many tweets along the lines: 'I can make you rich in seven days' – but would you say this directly, without introduction or further evidence, in any other business situation? Or should you describe yourself as an IT expert, for example, just because you can work your laptop? We don't think so!

Many people offer advice on web etiquette (netiquette) generally. We won't be suggesting hard-and-fast rules on Twitter or elsewhere. Isn't the very nature of social media somewhat subjective, casual, organic and evolving?

That said, how do you react to these scenarios? For example, do you automatically thank new followers for following you? On the one hand, it seems a nice thing to do. On the other hand, when you have lots of followers, acknowledgment can be clearly done on autopilot and/or outsourced. Then it's impersonal – and replies can seem like spam. But thanking people for retweets (RTs) where they pass your tweet post on to followers or 'favorite' it (keep it on file), is a way of showing you value this implied support.

Wishing people a happy national holiday, for example, can be a very genuine and audience-specific post that embraces the importance of the local splash of colour. You really do get a sense of the faces behind the businesses. It also helps you develop empathy (always a good thing) and build strong bridges with your words.

Other 'twitter-writing language' includes emoticons such as ☺ or :) and #Hashtags which introduce topics of general interest and are searchable, to enable users to research a theme. Because business users generally can't afford to be as flippant as other users, hashtags can help to qualify whether your tweet is light-hearted, for example

#JustSaying. Or you can target business readership with hashtags such as #BusinessCommunication or #globalprojects.

All these points lead to many companies instructing employees to express in their biography (bio) whether they are tweeting in a personal or company capacity and whether retweets are endorsements or not. It's essential to understand which voice to use at any given time – and also when to shout out, when to discuss, when to promote ideas, when to whisper, and when just to listen.

Here are some more tips.

First, timing is absolutely crucial – on two levels. The first relates to developing a sense of when to tweet and when not to. For instance, say it's Christmas and your business has great deals to rake in customers. So, just as you would normally advertise this information around 6–8 weeks before December, the month of Christmas, start tweeting about the deals then. On the second level, post your tweets in the right time zone for your potential global readers. It may be fruitless to post a fantastic offer in the early hours of their morning. Twitter is fast-moving and transient – your tweets will probably never be read by much of your target audience if you don't take this factor on board.

But just because tweeting is free, don't fill the timeline with incessant promotional tweets. This often puts followers off and they may 'unfollow' your business, opting out of further interaction.

So, how could you write the tweets using the example of Christmas deals? Perhaps like this:

> Have you started thinking about what to get for Christmas? So have we! www.indexgifts.co.uk

Or, maybe:

> Only 8 weeks to go till Christmas! Check out our great deals here: www.indexgifts.co.uk

As with Facebook Pages, use engaging tone, empathizing with your target audience and getting a balance between:

- promoting your business;
- interacting with your followers correctly;
- reacting to situations so that your organization is visible in the way you want;
- encouraging advocacy, which can have more credibility than self-promotion.

Second, when you write a business report or presentation, do you talk about your personal life? Probably not. So why tweet something like 'I had cornflakes for breakfast this morning' from your business Twitter account? Unless you can relate this to your business in some way (for example if your business produces breakfast cereals), it's best not to get banal here. Your followers won't expect it.

Finally, let's look at the quality of your writing. Yes, the 140 character limit promotes simplicity. But you'd better get the message right! Use shortened spellings with care (or avoid them, though that's not always possible, or expected). And wrong or no punctuation, or no capital letters at the beginning of sentences or with proper nouns (names of people and places) will just not do. For example, this is far from ideal:

Plz come 2 c our fab display show on fri 14 nov @ 8pm in vauxhall, south ldn. Details r here bit.ly/TCSQ12

Even if your target audience is fluent in such 'text speak', writing this way doesn't give a professionally credible impression to your followers.

Activity

Assuming you can understand it, how would you rewrite the last tweet example in 140 characters? Write your answer here.

_____

_____

_____

Using LinkedIn to promote or share information

LinkedIn is slightly different from Facebook and Twitter. It has clearer specifications. It's a professional network where all matters related to business, careers and employment are discussed and strictly professional connections are made. This makes networking with a business purpose easier: it's what LinkedIn is for – although its groups discourage blatant self-promotion or outright selling. It provides a business-to-consumer environment where you present yourself as *an expert* directly to particular customers, rather than to businesses.

Make use of the groups here for further targeting. Perhaps offer snippets of information where you hold back some detail, so that readers actually approach you – the known expert – for more.

If you analyse the writing people use, it's clearly geared to the audience. So jargon may be acceptable, up to a point. You'll see posts which are at face value acceptable for user-group purpose, such as: 'Can anyone help me with an urgency importance matrix?' (Human Resources Group); or 'What are the merits of phones or tablets as media consumption devices?' (Technology Group).

Interestingly, you'll notice many businesses use group discussions not just to get answers, but also to get more attention. They become the 'influencers', not necessarily because they persuade people to do things, but because their writing 'makes more noise.' This is in the sense that it starts and maintains discussions to which readers can relate – and respond.

So how can you design writing that does this? Well, for a start, try becoming a style detective as we've suggested in earlier chapters. For example, LinkedIn has just released a list of the most-shared articles of the past year. And what do we find? The top-runners are about how to work better. So among the top six, we find these four attention-grabbing business titles:

- 9 Things That Motivate Employees More Than Money;
- Steve Jobs and The Seven Rules of Success;
- Four Destructive Myths Most Companies Still Live By;
- 5 Things to do Every Day for Success.

The world will undoubtedly move on but, at this point, these are the words and tips that people want to share. Go with the trend – but also adapt your writing when the trends change, as they will.

To help you, we have some other suggestions too:

- As in traditional PR, try to use a topical subject of general or specific interest, as an anchor to promote discussion. If you have an expert insight into the problem, for example, bring this out in the discussion, without openly self-promoting or selling.

- It can also be useful to talk about the latest this, the newest that – 'early adoption' is a prime mover and shaker on the social media scene.

- Use word power to make impact, along the lines we showed you in Chapter 7 – to design an interesting, attention-grabbing headline.

Do you remember we showed in Chapter 7 how even negative words can be used to make justifiable business impact? Thus we can see that although two of the four most-shared articles listed above have the *positive* power word 'success' in the title, one has a *negative* power word 'destructive' to make us want to read on. This is the sort of thing we want you to look out for. Notice how others write to get our interest. Pick up practical tips every day – and build up your dossier of good examples.

Members can also share posts to and from Facebook and Twitter, allowing you to make full use of the formal or informal environments that social networking media provide. Indeed, one of the reasons why the phenomena are so popular is because users find their psychological selves relax when they're logged on. They can 'be themselves' more, finding a balance between facilitating social media networking on professional matters, but keeping a casual, informal feel too.

Business writing tips for LinkedIn profiles

The main difference between LinkedIn and other sites like Facebook and Twitter is that much of the information is about you: your skills, qualifications, work experience, career graph, the input you have in the job you do, or the business you run. So, it becomes very important to complete as many details as you can on your profile page. Use the same professionalism and proficiency you do when you write or update your CV.

For example, you could use a list approach to help you maintain the precision required for professional documentation like this.

Joe Smith
CEO, Whizzbang Services Ltd.
Newsham, United Kingdom | Information Technology

Current post: (*Enter details of your present job position*)

Past: (*Enter three (if you can) job positions you have held, starting with the most recent and usually moving in reverse chronological order, though this does not hold true for all countries. Do check.*)

Education: (*Enter your academic qualifications, usually starting with the most recent and moving in reverse chronological order*)

As you see, the format is very similar to that of a CV, but you get the added benefits of LinkedIn prompting you to fill in details you may otherwise have missed.

After you proceed to fill in links to your social networking media pages (for example Twitter profiles, blog sites and company or personal websites), you need to fill in the Summary, Specialities and Experience sections as you would do in your CV. Indeed, did you know LinkedIn has a CV uploading tool? If you upload your CV onto this, LinkedIn processes it into its profile template, checking if you then need to make any corrections. When technology is there to help us, we might as well use it, right?

When it comes to the actual words you write, a word of caution. LinkedIn has just conducted a review of millions of users' profile pages – and found that, in 2011, 'creative' was the most-used word. It's easy to see that if almost everyone describes themselves as *creative*, the word loses impact.

A similar thing is happening with words such as '*effective, organizational, innovative, problem solving, dynamic, motivated*'. You may have to think of different words to set you apart and promote brand you. Regularly revisit the activity you started in Chapter 7. The right words for today may have to change next year, and the year after that, and so on. But always remember, choose them carefully: you have to deliver what you write. There are also lists of the words that positively annoy readers, such as the management speak we highlighted in Chapter 8, so take note of those too.

Activity

Fill in the following sections here and consider uploading this information on to LinkedIn. You may want to get a friend or colleague to see if it reads well.

Summary:

Specialities:

Experience: (Make sure the order is the same as you have stated in the 'Past' section above)

Job 1:

Job 2:

Job 3:

Job 4:

Fill in details of your academic qualifications, usually in reverse chronological order, and do respond to LinkedIn prompters. They are crucial in helping you get the most out of this networking site, in terms of business. Make sure your writing style is sufficiently formal and to the point, and that your tone is warm yet serious. Here's an example.

Summary

Experienced and proficient in writing feature articles for newspapers and websites.

Excellent communicator with people of various ages and backgrounds.

Strong organizational, ICT and presentation skills.

A dedicated, proficient lecturer in journalism, mass communications and general humanities.

A caring and enthusiastic teaching assistant in mainstream and specialist schools.

Specialities

Lecturing in journalism and psychology at further and higher education levels; writing poetry and feature articles.

When writing for LinkedIn, remember that empty boxes simply will not do. Just as gaps that are unaccounted for in a CV lead to a patchy impression of a candidate by potential employers, so do empty sections in a LinkedIn profile.

The company blog – how useful is it really?

The word *blog* is actually short for 'weblog' (an online account of one's thoughts, findings, ideas and discussions, usually updated on a daily, weekly or monthly basis). Blogs cover all sorts of topics, for example diaries, recipes, movies, photography, technology and music.

A company blog (also known as a *corporate blog*, especially in the United States) is simply the blog section on a business organization's website. Professionals generally blog to update their customer base on business developments within their organization. Professionals from some cultures even include funny anecdotes, sometimes as a strategy to reflect the strong camaraderie between work colleagues. It gives the impression of an organization with a positive, friendly, working atmosphere and work culture. Have you seen this? Would it work for your organization and/or your culture?

Business writing tips for company blog posts

Blogs are very much based on one-to-many communication. They differ from traditional printed articles, as blogs can be written by anyone from 'the many'. It's a fascinating development: everyone now has a voice, so everyone can be a writer. But it doesn't necessarily mean that everybody can write well. That's why we're trying to give you as many tips as possible, so that you certainly do!

Blogs should, overall, still read like articles and inform. Their structure follows the medium of the internet. While printed material has to explain background within the articles themselves, blogs have the useful facility of linking to helpful information online. Make sure you supply links as part of your writing.

Keep your paragraphs shorter than in print. As we've mentioned earlier, reading on-screen can be tiring, so try to keep the length to one or two screens. Involve readers by inviting comments and consider interactive applications such as voting buttons.

You'll notice that bloggers use emoticons from time to time. The frequency depends on how professional the writer needs to appear, and how he or she needs to adapt style for the audience. The tricky point with blogs is that it's very easy to relax the tone, style, layout and presentation of your writing. While this is fine (and even a requisite) with personal blogs, be careful with your company blog posts. Here's an example.

G'Day Folks! We've had a tough time getting the mechanics of our next edition of the *i-car* to work, for the past couple of weeks, but it now appears we're making a breakthrough!

Watch this space for more...

While the overall feel of this post is cheerful and warm, the writing here a) is a bit too informal and b) doesn't match the news being delivered. Visitors will be quick to notice that the team hasn't reached the breakthrough. While some may be hooked because they want to know what it is, others may be put off and not return.

Taking the same example, let's rewrite it.

Hello everybody

As we have told you in our recent posts, we have been struggling with a couple of issues in the mechanics of our latest edition of the *i-car*. However, after much thinking, prodding and probing, we are about to make an exciting breakthrough that could potentially revolutionize the auto-engineering industry globally!

As you can see, the style is less informal yet friendly enough. The writing reflects the tone of the post; that is, the struggle involved in reaching the breakthrough and the consequent excitement in coming up with a potential industrial change.

Alongside addressing the style, tone and structure of your company blog posts, you also need to remember technical elements such as frequency of posts (for example are there daily updates, weekly entries, monthly accounts), length of posts (whether there is a set word limit or not), use of audio-visual aids (for example images, audio or video clips) and methods of giving feedback.

Some writing tips for when you use images and video

If marketing tools such as brochures, leaflets and pamphlets can have photos, why shouldn't websites, blogs and social networking media accounts have them as well? Relevant images can enhance whatever it is you are promoting to your target audience. Videos can be particularly effective and increasingly expected, not just by the young but across generations and cultures. Thanks to YouTube and camera phones, uploading audio-visual content is extremely easy, especially for sites such as Google+.

One of this site's USPs is its Hangout section, specifically designed for members to hang out and chat via webcams. Note the informality of the language: wouldn't this be a great place for your business to 'hang out' as it were, and interact with users and customers discussing feedback on your product or service? Of course, you would have to get this facility manned and also write Facebook posts and tweets to show you're available on Google+ for real-time video chatting. This could really put your business bang on the map of social media networking!

But be careful how you write any captions and text to create links to images and video clips. Misleading text almost always puts customers off. If you're advertising a bargain, make sure it is one. Also hyperlinks have to create interest. Do you think this one does?

> CLICK HERE TO SEE OUR CEO'S SPEECH AT THE LAUNCH OF OUR NEW I-CAR

First, why is the text written in upper case? It's nothing much to shout about as it stands! Second, when was the launch? Why should visitors hear the speech? Was it inspirational? How? All these questions need to be answered in order for the hyperlink to get lots of hits.

Activity

Using these pointers, rewrite the text of the hyperlink here.

_____

_____

Conclusion

This chapter has shown you how companies write for social media platforms for different reasons. They are largely to do with a desire to get individuals to help them get their name out there – even go viral – to develop and maintain a good global reputation.

Remember, never write to offend or damage anyone else's reputation, because defamation cases are now appearing as well as other legal aspects of writing on social media, read globally. Even if there's no legislation where you are, there may be laws and customs to think of in other countries.

Your writing has to be very user-oriented, with interesting information which you hope fans will share with their friends, so that information is passed on in a snowballing effect. In terms of how you actually write, think of an appealing gift (the information you are presenting) and wrap it attractively (in the language you use).

As the writing style used on the new media is mostly very upbeat (occasionally even flippant at first sight), this can seem at odds with other more traditional areas of business writing. This is one reason why we suggest throughout the book that companies probably need to look with 'new eyes' at their writing as a whole. Adapting their style to suit the new media may mean adapting their style elsewhere too, so as not to lose corporate identity, or otherwise confuse readers with a glaring mismatch of writing styles.

Worksheet

Section A: Knowing your theory

Based on what you have understood from this chapter, respond to the following questions and statements by ticking the 'Yes' or 'No' boxes.

	Yes	No
1 Are social networking media changing the way we communicate personally and professionally?	☐	☐
2 When understood and used strategically can social networking media become platforms for the global promotion of corporate identities?	☐	☐
3 Being effective in social media is all about direct selling.	☐	☐
4 Does your text need to be engaging in tone and quality to get more 'Likes' on your Facebook Page?	☐	☐
5 Is 'text speak' the only way to communicate with young audiences?	☐	☐
6 Tweeting incessantly for the purposes of promoting your business is akin to spamming the Twitter timeline.	☐	☐
7 Company blog posts should only be formal in tone and structure.	☐	☐
8 Is LinkedIn a professional social networking medium which can promote both you – the professional – and your company?	☐	☐

Section B: Business at leisure

This chapter has taken an in-depth look into how we increasingly use social networking media to promote our businesses and ourselves from a computer, tablet device or smartphone screen. We've also given you several examples and tips on how to improve your use of global business English when using social networking media as a marketing tool to grow your business and/or maximize your profile.

The following exercise lists some activities. Some might not apply to you right now, some probably do, or may in the future – try the ones that are relevant to you.

- Does your company have a Facebook page? If so, take a look at it. If not, take a look at another company's page. In light of the tips we have given, how would you improve the business writing on it?

- Do you have a Twitter account? If so, looking at our suggestions on writing tweets, what changes would you make so that Twitter works better for your business?

- What changes would you make to any company blog you currently have? Would you write posts more frequently or less? Would you include audio or video content to complement your writing? Have you any other thoughts about this?

- What would you write if you had to raise awareness about your company and its product or service through posts using the Groups facility on LinkedIn?

Chapter Thirteen
Quality matters

Using English well can be the difference between winning and losing in business today.

Why it matters to get it right

Any organization that believes in consistently producing quality products and services knows this means getting things right, first and every time. This should apply to business communication too, shouldn't it?

It's a fact that each piece of business writing you send out can be – indeed, will be – quality assessed by someone, somewhere. It may be within the organization or it may be by external readers, who are even unknown to you.

In a sense, your written words are 'frozen' at the point of time in which you wrote them. If they are wrong, once you put them out into cyberspace, you can never actually retrieve them. Yes, you can issue corrections but your original mistakes remain untouched, out there for all to see. And even if your written communication is not wrong, in the sense that it has no mistakes, it may be *wrong for purpose*, as we showed in step 1 in our global word power skills guide in Chapter 8.

Making mistakes is human, isn't it?

We cannot deny it: we're all capable of making writing mistakes every day. Whoever we are, whatever we do, whatever our proficiency in business English (or any other language in fact), it is part of the human condition to make errors.

Making mistakes may not be foolish in your first draft – but what is foolish is not to take corrective action, so readers don't see those errors. If quality matters to you, that is. Then you should make sure you remove mistakes, as far as humanly possible, before they go live.

A really useful tip to help you achieve better results in business English writing is to *expect your writing to be wrong*. This may sound negative but if you think about it, by expecting your writing to be wrong, you're more likely to be in a position:

1 To see any mistakes that may be there.

2 Then to take these mistakes out of your writing before you send it.

3 To present a totally professional corporate and personal image.

Checking – even double checking – your writing before you send it can pay great dividends. It may mean you spend a little bit longer at the planning stage, but isn't it time worth investing in your success? Isn't it better to raise the odds that each message you send is right? Isn't the perception of a professional 'brand you' worth the effort? Don't your readers deserve that too?

Written mistakes – the impact on readers and businesses

We know that making mistakes in business writing matter, the world over, because bosses mention it, customers mention it, stakeholders mention it, and so do the public at large. Maybe finance directors should get involved in spreading the message, to drive the point home. Maybe they should be sending all staff in their organizations a stark message about *the cost* to business of slipshod communication. They could highlight this inescapable fact:

> Business writing mistakes (including errors and unclear, confusing or alienating messages) can = lost cash + lost custom + lost goodwill + loss of reputation = reduced profits and/or regional or global competitiveness.

Mistakes in general

'Whats wrong with errors, if I do my job well?' people often ask. That's the crux of the matter really: will readers think you do your job well, if they see mistakes? It's unfortunate, but if you make written mistakes, some readers will focus on these – at the expense of what else you may be saying.

There were two deliberate mistakes in the last paragraph. Did you spot them?

We wrote *'whats'* for what's and *'errers'* for errors. If you did spot them did you do a double-take and focus on them?

Many readers do focus on mistakes. Whether you like it or not, bosses, customers and readers generally, make value judgements, such as: 'This writer is simply not professional enough.' And the trouble for that writer is that, in a hard-pressed job market, the people who write well will always have the competitive edge.

Whether it's fair or not, readers can also view mistakes as direct evidence of sloppy business performance in general. External customers, in particular, can point the finger of blame not just at the individual writer who has written poorly, but at whole teams – even at the company as a whole. This case study demonstrates what we mean.

CASE STUDY Customer service feedback at an international airport

The authorities at a major international airport hub decided to run a customer feedback survey. Their intentions were admirable: they genuinely wanted to see how they could improve their services to customers.

The airport's senior managers outsourced the survey to an external marketing agency. This agency designed a form to invite positive comments as well as negative feedback.

So far, so good: the senior managers eagerly awaited the results. They knew all feedback would not be favourable. That's the name of the game: to stay successful, organizations know they must continuously improve. That's why they commissioned the survey.

But imagine their overwhelming disappointment at some of the responses they saw. Why were they disappointed? It was because many of the negative reactions featured things for which the airport had not felt responsible.

You see, there was a deluge of complaints about typographical errors made by the marketing agency to which the airport had subcontracted the survey. A surprisingly high number of customers were irritated enough by what they perceived as lack of professionalism on the part of the airport that they criticized the mistakes openly. Many sent the forms back with the errors encircled in pen.

These respondents largely omitted to comment on the operational aspects and customer service generally – areas that the airport had hoped to address.

A difficult lesson was nonetheless learnt by the senior managers. Written mistakes matter. Customers made that very clear. For them, mistakes implied poor performance and customer disservice throughout the organization. Although in this instance, the airport's staff had not written the mistakes, the errors reflected on them – and not on the agency. For future surveys, they realized that their communication could never be fully outsourced: they, the clients, had to retain the ultimate responsibility.

What's more, mistakes are not just about poor spelling, grammar and punctuation. Mistakes can be a direct result of staff not thinking logically, nor anticipating likely outcomes each time they send out a written message.

Here's a practical example that we've seen in the last week, as we write.

CASE STUDY

A multinational company arranged a conference call between global teams. The e-mail notification correctly identified the conference date; the timing had been converted correctly for the different time zones involved; the right people had been notified and were in place waiting for the call. And can you guess why the call didn't take place as planned? Nobody knew which conference dialling number or code to use.

If a writer leaves essential information out of written communication, this counts as a mistake too.

Getting your written messages right can also be about understanding how to write positively, cutting out jargon, ambiguity and rudeness. Even when you have to communicate negative messages, there are ways of softening the blow and developing empathy. Imagine, for example, you have to write an e-mail to a customer who has asked if she can have an extra discount for a bulk order of your product. Imagine how the customer would feel if the main message in your reply is as follows:

No, we cannot offer you a volume discount. It is not company policy to do this.

On the level of customer service, this sentence is wrong – even though it's grammatically correct English. It undermines the quality of the service you are providing if you don't express some sort of empathy. Maybe you cannot offer an extra volume discount but you can still express an element of customer service, for example:

We are very sorry that we cannot offer any discounts. However, we can assure you that we make every effort to keep our prices as competitive as we can, as our customers' interests mean everything to us.

At times, quality writing may mean more, not fewer words. In all its manifestations, quality is about investing in future success, and there is no quick fix.

Our writing can determine whether we make a great impact or a damaging impact; whether we win or lose custom; whether we foster goodwill or alienate those we should be supporting. If poor business English writing prevails in the global workplace and causes confusion, misunderstandings or missed opportunities, then it's easy to see how great writing will set you apart – and underpin your professionalism.

Activity

Have you come across mistakes in corporate communication recently? Jot down any that you can recall. How did you react when you saw them? Do you think they affected the company's performance or reputation? If so, in what way?

_____

_____

_____

_____

_____

Quality: The debate is on

It's extremely interesting to find that different people, different cultures and different organizations can all have a varying perspective on what quality means. This is especially true when it comes to business communication.

As an illustration, a newly-appointed senior Asian manager in a major oil company had, in his team, a number of Asian and European staff for whom English was a second language. Although the manager was not fluent in spoken English himself, he felt he was more fluent than the rest of his team. When it came to writing, he felt that, though far from perfect, he was still better than most. So, in his view, the quality of his English was adequate and therefore fit for purpose.

Now this is in stark contrast to a view expressed by a senior Dutch manager in a multinational energy company that uses English as its common business language. In his opinion, his non-English staff must try to speak and write almost flawless English, at all times. He sets the bar high and it must never be lowered. Maybe this is a reflection of the Dutch education system which places great emphasis on foreign language learning, as the Netherlands is proud of its prowess as a global trading nation.

So you can see that if we talk about quality business writing, organizations need a view on what this means in terms of their business communication. Does it mean _top_ quality or _acceptable_ quality? It's quite fascinating to find that some organizations will settle for a _satisfactory_ quality rating, rather than _excellent_. What do you think your organization expects? Which viewpoint do you personally favour? And shouldn't customers' views be taken into account too?

Let's use the following extract as part of the debate as to how many mistakes affect quality. As it's unfair to take any one website and analyse its mistakes, we've instead put together a number of real-life business English errors from different sources. You can see what they look like from a reader's perspective.

Look at this passage, which has been composed from extracts from real-life training companies' websites across the world:

CASE STUDY Inter-national training at it's best

Adiding by our well-received principhes of quality and based on years of successful internatonal expereince, we deliver bespoke workshops and infididual coaching on reguest.

This, our training websize, was launched in 2002. To find out more about our mangement consultancy servces visit our Group webside at....

If you require any further detials please leave a massage for us in the contact box provided.

How did you react to this writing? Did the company come across as professional and credible? Are these trainers the 'best,' as they suggest? When there are so many first-class, apparently mistake-free professionals to choose from, would you buy from this training company as your first choice?

Are you surprised to know that some of the websites we reviewed, at random, had up to 12 written business English mistakes in a similar length of text? Did you spot the 14 errors in this one? Here is the correct version:

CASE STUDY International training at its best

Abiding by our well-received principles of quality and based on years of successful international experience, we deliver bespoke workshops and individual coaching on request.

This, our training website, was launched in 2002. To find out more about our management consultancy services visit our Group website at....

If you require any further details, please leave a message for us in the contact box provided.

Activity

Gather a selection of your organization's written documentation, or you could take a selection from another organization you come across. What quality rating would you give each individual item, expressed in marks out of 10 – and why? Then work out what the overall average rating would be.

If it's your company's documentation you have looked at, are you pleased with the result? Is the rating you gave the same as the rating you personally would hope to achieve?

_____

_____

_____

Some common business writing errors in global English

There are lots of blogs and lists that people forward via social media highlighting the most common errors in business writing today. We suggest you take a look at these if you care about maintaining quality in your business writing, as we hope you do.

We'll be touching on some grammar tips in Chapter 14 as one way of helping you avoid mistakes. Here's a small sample of frequently encountered general mistakes we find in a global business English context. These can also affect the quality of what you write:

- **eg and ie.** eg is the abbreviation of the Latin phrase *exempli gratia* and means 'for example.' ie is the abbreviation of the Latin phrase *id est* and means 'that is' or 'that is to say'.

  People often interchange these abbreviations wrongly. Do watch out for this, as it can affect meaning significantly. To help you see the difference, look at this real-life sentence we found: '*Our standard discount applies, eg 10%.*' This is a mistake that undermines a quality, professional image. If the discount is standard, then 10% is a precise, definite discount – not an example of a possible discount. The correct wording has to be: '*Our standard discount applies, ie 10%.*'

  Can you see the problem in the next sentence? '*Some fonts, ie Verdana, have been designed to use on the web.*' As Verdana is just one example of a font that has been designed for use on the web, the writer should have used *eg* not *ie*: '*Some fonts, eg Verdana, have been designed to use on the web.*'

- **When and if.** Many non-native English writers have difficulty understanding the distinction between these two words. Generally speaking, 'when' means 'at which time' or 'in which situation' or 'during the time that'. It has a concrete feel to it, even though it sometimes refers to the future. 'If' on the other hand, is conditional. It feels more tentative. It supposes something will happen, that's in turn likely to make something else happen.

  Examples are:

1 'If my train is on time, I will be in Paris in two hours' (UK English).

2 'When my train is on time, I will be in Paris in two hours' (typical non-native English variant).

Native English writers would not write sentence 2. They intuitively build in the conditional clause: 'if one thing happens' (that is, 'the train arrives on time') 'then the second thing will result' (that is, 'I will be in Paris in two hours'). The second thing depends on the first.

Are you now able to see which of the following sentences is 'more English'?

1 'If it's not a problem, I will visit you tomorrow.'

2 'When it is not a problem, I will visit you tomorrow.'

It is sentence 1, based on the same reasoning: if the first condition is met (that is, 'it is not a problem') then the second thing will happen ('I will visit you tomorrow').

- **May and can.** The verb 'can' in English is used to express ability – or being allowed to do something. It is definite in meaning. For example: 'I can speak Spanish' is the same as 'I am able to speak Spanish'.

    The verb 'may' is used to express possibility. For example: 'I may learn Spanish or Mandarin Chinese' tells us the speaker is not yet able to speak either language but is *thinking about* learning one of them.

    'May' is also used to ask permission in a polite way, for example: 'May I go with you?' or 'May I have a cup of coffee, please?' Having said that, it is quite normal for business peers to say or write 'Can we talk about this? Can I attend the meeting?'

- **Borrow and lend.** If you borrow something you take and use something that belongs to someone else (on the understanding that you will return it). For example: 'As it's raining and I have to dash to my next meeting in town, please may I borrow your umbrella? I'll give it back to you tomorrow.'

    If you 'lend' something you give it to someone to use (on the understanding they will return it). Thus the person who *owned* the umbrella we just referred to, *lent* it to the person who *borrowed* it for short-term use, to get to the meeting dry.

- **Homonyms.** These are two or more words that sound the same but have different spellings and meanings. They can confuse native and non-native English writers alike.

    Two such words that are frequently confused are 'principal' and 'principle'. 'Principal' is an adjective generally meaning first in importance; also a noun meaning: a chief or senior person; an original sum of money for investment. This should not be confused with 'principle', which is a noun meaning a fundamental truth or quality; a rule or belief governing a person's morally correct behaviour and attitudes.

Activity

Do any of these examples trip you or your colleagues up? Are there any others you can think of? You may care to list them here – and take the opportunity of brushing up your skills in how to use them.

_____

_____

_____

_____

_____

To deal or not to deal with other people's mistakes

Company guidance can be useful to let staff know what to do, if anything, about written mistakes they see others send. Naturally enough, it's a topic that needs to be handled sensitively – especially where native speakers receive written material containing mistakes made by their foreign counterparts. Might it be wrong to undermine non-native English writers' confidence, when they're making great efforts to communicate in another language? Or is it better to correct their mistakes in a positive, supportive way, as mistakes can affect a company's reputation?

Here's our advice. Try to put in place an office culture where it's seen as a strength to ask (as we've seen throughout, this may come more naturally to some cultures than others). And offer support if your staff are routinely getting things wrong.

Maintaining a mistake-free zone

Proofreading tips

A golden rule to help you maintain quality is to expect mistakes in your writing. Check everything you write before you send it out. Choose ways to help you from the following tips:

- Allow sufficient time for your proofreading. If you rush, you may still overlook the mistakes you are looking for.

- If the subject matter is, for example, a challenging technical or legal document, it can be easier to proofread on paper than on a computer screen. We are naturally eco-conscious and don't encourage unnecessary printing, but sometimes it prevents further iteration to get things right sooner rather than later.

- Use a standard or online dictionary or grammar book to help you, or your computer's spelling or grammar checker (set on the correct variant of English for your target audience). Do be aware that this is not failsafe. It may let the wrong words through, especially homophones (as we've mentioned, words which sound the same, although the meanings and spellings can be different): 'brake' for 'break', 'there' for 'their' etc.

- You could try reading your lines backwards (people sometimes use a ruler to read one line at a time, to avoid distraction). This won't help you check meaning but you can check that the words are spelt correctly.

- Check for meaning and logical arrangement.

- Almost everyone trips over some words. Make a self-help list of any words you regularly get wrong so that you can check them quickly and effectively next time you write them.

Summary

This chapter has been about helping you understand that every writing task ideally needs to contribute to factors such as personal, team and company success. Every piece of written communication you put out that contains mistakes has the potential to undermine quality, professionalism, credibility and reputation.

Avoid that risk by focusing on getting your communication right each time. Realize that quality business writing involves being correct on many levels, following the principles set out in the global word power skills guide in Chapter 8.

Worksheet

Section A: Knowing your theory

Based on what you have understood from this chapter, respond to the following questions and statements by ticking the 'Yes' or 'No' boxes.

	Yes	No
1 Once you put words out into cyberspace, can you ever retrieve them?	☐	☐
2 Double-checking your writing before sending it can pay great dividends.	☐	☐
3 Can mistakes be made if staff don't think logically and don't anticipate likely outcomes before they send a message?	☐	☐
4 Can different people, different cultures and different organizations have a varying perspective on what quality means?	☐	☐
5 Do the abbreviations 'eg' and 'ie' mean the same?	☐	☐
6 The verb 'may' is used to express ability, while the verb 'can' is used to express possibility.	☐	☐
7 Should you offer support if your staff keep getting things wrong?	☐	☐
8 Is proofreading just about finding typographical errors?	☐	☐

Section B: It's quality control time!

In this chapter, we have emphasized the importance of professional quality and standards in global business English writing. We've also reminded you to use the global word power skills system shown in Chapter 8 (which includes checking for any mistakes that need correcting before business writing is sent out). So, in the following sentences, can you identify the mistakes and correct them, and/or identify any areas for possible change and make changes?

1 Dear Mr Matthews, You have a payment demanded by us for $1700. The invoice of your billings is attached herewith.

Tip: Maybe the language used here could do with a little makeover.

Your version for your readers:

2 The company's ethical quality requests you to deliver all goods in FairTrade packaging.

Tip: Something seems wrong with the terminology and grammar used here.

Your version for your readers:

3 I am highly stressing as the third quarter report has made no progress by us and the figures are regressing.

Tip: How could you improve the clarity of this sentence?

Your version for your readers:

4 The tag line for our anti-smoking advertisement campaign would be 'Kill Smoking!'

Tip: Can you think of a better tag line?

> Your version for your readers:

5 Our staff must adhere to our corporate discipline policy or else will face a disciplinary.

Tip: This could be expressed better. Can you think how?

> Your version for your readers:

Chapter Fourteen
Writing tips for everyday business

Professionalism matters in writing, as in every aspect of your business performance.

Punctuation and grammar in global English

As you know, this book isn't an English language primer but this chapter does just highlight why punctuation, grammar and other writing conventions matter from a business perspective. We mention topics that multinational companies have asked us to cover in training workshops. If you're confident about the subject already, you may wish to move on. Or you might like to share some of the tips with your colleagues.

Punctuation matters

It's easy to see why punctuation matters in your business writing, by taking a look at an extract of what *unpunctuated* writing looks like, as follows.

> mr jones the companys hr director needed an update on the latest recruitment drive he wanted to know whether the online application system was working reports had filtered through that all was not going to plan a colleague explained that candidates were certainly experiencing problems as the systems had crashed and in her opinion it would be better to extend the closing date would he be prepared to authorize this

Even native English speakers find it difficult to make sense of this at a glance. Indeed every reader will have to work at 'decoding' the message, whatever their proficiency in English. That's why punctuation is intended to help readers understand writing more easily. There are a number of ways of punctuating the extract. Here's one suggestion.

> Mr Jones, the company's HR Director, needed an update on the latest recruitment drive. He wanted to know whether the online application system was working.
>
> Reports had filtered through that all was not going to plan.
>
> A colleague explained that candidates were certainly experiencing problems, as the systems had crashed. In her opinion, it would be better to extend the closing date. Would he be prepared to authorize this?

Punctuation has made the extract much easier to read. That's how useful punctuation can be, on one level. Sometimes punctuation also helps readers understand different meanings, as these two sentences show:

Li, our Managing Director has arrived in Beijing.
Li, our Managing Director, has arrived in Beijing.

In the first sentence, the writer is telling a person (named Li) that the Managing Director (name unknown) has arrived in Beijing. In the second sentence, the writer informs readers (names unknown) that the Managing Director (named Li) has arrived in Beijing.

Punctuation marks expressed in English

In the digital economy, even work areas that appear to be voice-driven, for example contact centres, need to relay messages for written e-mail follow-up if they are to operate successfully. For this reason, we are sometimes asked the names for English terms and symbols used to express punctuation marks. Table 14.1 shows the most common.

TABLE 14.1

Term	Symbol	Term	Symbol
Capital letters (or upper case):	**A,B,C (etc)**	Hyphen or dash	-
Lower case	**a, b, c (etc)**	Slash (or stroke)	/
Comma	,	Brackets	( )
Full stop (UK English) or period (UK and US English) or dot	.	Ampersand	&
Speech or double quotation marks or inverted commas	" "	Square brackets	[ ]
Speech or single quotation marks or inverted commas	' '	At sign	@
Question mark	?	Semicolon	;
Exclamation mark	!	Colon	:
Apostrophe	'	Asterisk	*
Hash or Hashtag (Twitter)	#	Underscore	_

Parts of speech

In English grammar, words can be categorized into *parts of speech*. These include nouns, pronouns, adjectives, verbs, adverbs, prepositions, conjunctions and interjections.

A noun names a person, place or thing,
    for example: girl, London, newspaper.

A pronoun is a word that can take the place of a noun and functions like it,
    for example: I, this, who, he, they.

An adjective is a word that describes a noun,
    for example: red, clear, clever.

A verb is a 'doing word' or describes a state of being,
    for example: write, run, work, be.

An adverb is a word that describes a verb,
    for example: fast, happily, later, urgently.

A preposition is a word that links a noun to another noun,
    for example: to, on, under, in.

A conjunction is a word that joins words or sentences,
    for example: and, but, or, so.

An interjection is a short exclamation often followed by an exclamation mark (!),
    for example: hi! oh!

Some other grammatical points of interest

A *comma* is generally used to signify a brief pause in a sentence. Very often, people wrongly use a comma to do the work of a full stop (or period). For example: 'I examined the computer, it had obviously been damaged.' As there are two complete statements in that sentence, not just a pause, one could use a full stop: 'I examined the computer. It had obviously been damaged.' A native English writer might use a conjunction and an extra verb to improve fluidity. For example: 'I examined the computer and found it had obviously been damaged.'

A comma is also used to link lists of items, groups of words, adjectives, actions and adverbs. For example: 'She listed the things she would need for her presentation: a laptop, a projector, screen, flipchart and marker pens.'

Apostrophes are used where one or more letters have been left out of a word. For example:

'I'm' is the contraction of 'I am'
'It's' is the contraction of 'it is' or 'it has'
'You'll' is the contraction of 'you will'

'The employee's rights' are the rights of one employee
'The employees' rights' are the rights of employees

The general rule is:

Apostrophe before the s ('s) indicates singular possession.
Apostrophe after the s (s') indicates plural possession.

Unfortunately, English always has some irregular forms, such as:

'men' is the plural of 'man' but the possessive is 'men's'
'children' is the plural of 'child' but the possessive is 'children's'
'its' is the possessive of 'it' – yet takes no apostrophe at all.

Forming plurals of nouns

Most nouns have a singular form (to denote one) and a plural (to denote more than one). The standard way of forming plurals from singular nouns is to add 's'. However, this does not always work, as in the case of 'child/ children'; 'lady/ladies'; 'foot/feet', to mention a few. So do refer to relevant English grammar resources if you need more help with this.

There's one challenge that arises very often. People often use an apostrophe followed by 's' when they write the plural of say, tomato. So they write 'tomato's' when it should be tomatoes. In business we routinely find people writing company's when they mean to write companies (plural). The word company's does exist, but it means 'of the company,' an entirely different meaning to the plural.

Vowels and consonants

In written English, 'a, e, i, o, u' are the standard vowels and the remaining letters in the alphabet are *consonants*.

The definite and indefinite article

The word 'the' is known as the definite article and exists in the same form in both singular and plural. The words 'a' and 'an' are known as the indefinite article and only exist in the singular. For the plural form, English uses the word 'some'.

If you are a non-native English writer, are you sometimes a bit puzzled as to when you use the definite or indefinite article? If so, you're not alone! To help you, here is a general guideline. Where you are referring to something in *general* use 'a' (before a word beginning with a consonant) or 'an' (before a word beginning with a vowel). Once again though, true to form in the English language, there are some exceptions, for example: 'an hotel'.

So, let's say a company receives an e-mail: 'Please can you let me know how long an order will take to deliver?' The company will see the question as tentative and non-specific. There is no order, only a general enquiry about how long it would take, if somebody were to place an order.

Now let's say the company receives this e-mail enquiry: 'Please can you tell me how long *the* order will take to deliver?' The word 'the' makes this enquiry appear more specific and we imagine it relates to an order that has already been placed.

Activity

Do you ever have any problems with any of the points of grammar we've outlined? Do your colleagues? Or are there any other points to add to the list? If so, it would be a good idea then to research the answers from colleagues who may know. Otherwise, check by using reputable grammar books or online resources.

_____

_____

_____

_____

_____

_____

_____

_____

Agreement of subject and verb

When a subject in a sentence is in the singular, then the verb must be in the singular too. When the subject is plural, then the verb is in the plural, in agreement with it. This is also called concord. Examples are:

> Paul is at university and so is his brother.
> Paul is at university and so are his brother and sister.

> They understand the reason why they have to do this.
> She understands the reasons why she has to do this and why you have to do it too.

> These conditions apply now.
> This condition applies now.

Non-native English writers can forget to check concord in their writing. Two quite typical examples are:

> Sara has received our e-mail. Has you received it too?
> (Correct version: Sara has received our e-mail. Have you received it too?)

> This kind of topics
> (Correct version: These kinds of topics)

As a rule of thumb: all you have to do is work out who is doing the action and make your verb relate to who or what is doing it, consistently. In some sentences you may have to refer back to check.

Question tags

Question tags (where words or phrases are added to sentences to make questions) are often used in conversation and now in e-mails too. As they encourage listeners or readers to respond, they can be very useful in global business English, not just to check language comprehension but to gauge reserved cultures' reactions as well.

Examples are:

It's a good outcome, isn't it?'
You don't have a meeting today, do you?
You can make it in time, can't you?

Incorrect usage examples are:

You have got the right files, isn't it?
He is wrong, doesn't he?
These kind of things are dealt with in your department, isn't it?

Correct versions are:

You have got the right files, haven't you?
He is wrong, isn't he?
These kinds of things are dealt with in your department, aren't they?

This tip should help you. Try balancing the same verb (including whether it is singular or plural) on either side of the sentence; then use a negative in the questioning part of the sentence, at its end.

Writing a date

Differing conventions

There are a number of correct ways of writing dates in English.

The UK English format (which most of Europe uses) is:
DD/MM/YY (where DD=day, MM=Month, YY=year)
This is in sharp contrast with the US format which is:
MM/DD/YY

and the format used in Japan, for example, which is:
YY/MM/DD

Not to understand the different conventions can create immense problems. If you have to book international transport, hotel accommodation or arrange deliveries, meetings and so on, you will know how important it is to know how to input the correct dates. When you write globally, it may not always help to default to a house style format. Glocal may be appropriate: you do need to understand the convention that customers use, alongside your own.

Check if there's any uncertainty at all, because being **successful** in business should be about embracing customers' needs, not about seeing clients as 'awkward' if they do something differently, not in your way!

Examples that are all perfectly acceptable in UK English are:

21 January 2013
21st January, 2013
21 Jan 2013
21st Jan. 2013
21/01/13

The format: '1st, 2nd, 3rd' uses an abbreviation that follows the spoken word. So we abbreviate 1st for 'first', 2nd for 'second', 3rd for 'third' – placing the final two letters of the word behind the number, and so on. It is a style that looks rather old-fashioned nowadays.

As we have mentioned, US English uses a month/day/year format and other countries can do the same. In this case, you would write:

January 21 2009
01/21/09

This particular date is not too problematic because we know that there are not 21 months in a year. But where readers do not understand the differences between the UK and US conventions, they could have problems with a date such as:

03/06/09

In the UK this denotes 3 June 2009 – but in the US denotes 6 March 2009.

Can you see how not understanding these differences in writing can create real misunderstandings, with serious commercial repercussions, such as getting deliveries wrong?

International date format

This helpful format makes dates understandable internationally. It goes like this:

YYYY- MM-DD
where
YYYY refers to all the digits (for example 2015)
MM refers to the month (01 to 12)
DD refers to the day (01 to 31)

Some confusions

Days and weeks

If you write 'next Tuesday', people can get confused as to whether you are referring to the first Tuesday that follows after the day you wrote this – or whether you mean a Tuesday in the next week. So, as an example, if you write it on a Monday, is 'next Tuesday' the next day (which we would take it to mean)? Or is it the Tuesday of the following week? If you write it on a Friday, it is easier to see that it would have to be the Tuesday of the following week.

'This coming Tuesday' has the same meaning as 'next Tuesday'. So do be careful. We know of instances where misunderstandings about this, led to missed appointments. Ironically, the people who misunderstand the correct use of the expression are the ones who can get angry about the confusion! Imagine the unnecessary cost if you book foreign travel for the wrong date. The best arrangement is always to write the precise date you mean, for example: 'Next Tuesday, 4th November.'

'In a couple of weeks' literally means: in two weeks, as 'a couple' means 'two' in English. It is true that 'a couple of weeks' can be used in a looser sense, meaning in about two weeks, but it is best to check. As another example, the Dutch expression: '*een paar dagen*' means a few days, but the Dutch often wrongly translate this into English as 'a couple', or 'two' days. So where orders are concerned, it's best to clarify what is meant in these instances.

'Next Monday week' means 'a week from next Monday'. 'Over a week' in English means in 'more than a week's time.' But non-native English writers often use the expression 'over a week' to mean in a week's time; that is, one week from now (for example 'The delivery will be over a week'). Again, be careful if you are dealing with orders, because you can confuse people.

'A fortnight' means two weeks. As many nationalities are unaware of this word, it can be better to avoid it. 'A long weekend' means a break of three to four days (that will cover a Saturday and Sunday and may start on a Friday and end on the following Monday).

Time off

In UK English, people usually refer to their 'holiday' where US English uses 'vacation'. Time off work for holidays is referred to as 'leave'; time off through illness is 'sick leave'; parents' time off from work when a baby is born is either 'maternity leave' (for the mother) or 'paternity leave' (for the father). Time off work may be 'paid leave' or 'unpaid leave' depending on circumstances.

Public or Bank holidays

A public holiday is an official holiday for the majority of a state or country. In the UK, the term 'Bank holiday' is used when the public holiday falls on a weekday when banks are closed by law. When you write about public holidays or Bank holidays globally, be aware that they can vary from country to country, usually being cultural in origin.

It can hold up your business communication not to research when different countries may have national holidays. Your orders and deliveries, for example, may be held up at foreign ports etc as a direct result.

Time

Things can go so very wrong in business when we fail to understand there are also differing conventions for expressing times. People fail to turn up to meetings at the right time, they miss flights, they miss deadlines: in short, if it's time-bound, it can go wrong! And let's face it, in business what isn't linked to time? Here are some guidelines to help.

UK English

All these written versions are correct in English:

The meeting starts at 09.00am.
The meeting starts at 9am (or 9 a.m.).
The meeting starts at nine o'clock in the morning.

The English use both the 12-hour clock (morning and afternoon) and the 24-hour clock (especially for timetables) so:

09.00 means nine o'clock in the morning.
21.00 means nine o'clock in the evening.
Strangely enough, 24.00 is also 0.00 hours.

Now if we write in English 'The meeting starts at half past eight' this could mean the meeting starts at 08.30 or 20.30. Often we will know from context: for example, if meetings are held during normal office hours then half past eight in the morning is the more likely time. But say we work in a staggered hours' working environment, then it could be a morning or an evening meeting. You need to clarify.

Differing conventions in different countries

There are even more differences to take into account. For example, in the United States generally the 24-hour clock is not used (except specifically by some professions, for example the military, the police and the medical profession). Some countries (for example Germany and the Netherlands) use a format to express half an hour before an hour. This is alien to native English writing – where half past six (6:30), for example, would be 'half seven' in the German, or Dutch way of thinking. Don't underestimate the problems you can run into when doing business globally, if you don't face up to this likely source of misunderstanding.

Activity

Are there any points in the sections about writing dates and times that you did not know about? Are there any that have proved a problem for you, or your organization in the past? Maybe you could extend this section yourself to cover writing numbers and other measurements that you may need to use? Wherever there may have been a problem, what did you do or what resources did you use to sort it out? Also, are there any points that you feel you should highlight to colleagues? If so, list the points here.

So, to conclude this chapter, can you see how punctuation serves the useful purpose of helping readers read messages and also helps highlight where the emphasis needs to go?

Grammar also helps you set out business writing into manageable, orderly sections that help readers understand your meanings. In many ways, we could say punctuation and grammar combined also help 'clothe our logic'. Used well, they aid the fluidity of your writing so that all the points *are seen to* add up into a coherent whole.

This chapter has additionally highlighted how things that may seem simple at first sight can easily lead to confusion if not communicated correctly. When you write for a global audience, ways of relaying factual information may not be straightforward. Getting it wrong can easily lead to misunderstandings, commercial disadvantage and unfortunate first impressions.

We should never underestimate the importance of building relationships. Something as seemingly small as not giving the right written presentation of time can lead to something as serious as not attending a meeting at the same time as your clients. We hope these tools will therefore equip you to maximize your business advantage.

Worksheet

Section A: Knowing your theory

Based on what you have understood from this chapter, respond to the following questions and statements by ticking the 'Yes' or 'No' boxes.

		Yes	No
1	Is punctuation intended to help readers understand writing more easily?	☐	☐
2	Is the following mark ';' called a colon and this ':' a semi-colon?	☐	☐
3	Is this mark '#' called a hash tag and this '*' an asterisk?	☐	☐
4	A noun names a person, place or object, while an adjective describes a noun.	☐	☐
5	Is a conjunction a word that joins sentences and a preposition a word that links one noun with another?	☐	☐
6	Does the term 'concord' refer to the agreement of the subject with the verb in a sentence?	☐	☐
7	Do different nationalities all use the same date and time conventions and interpret large numbers in one uniform way?	☐	☐
8	Is this mark '-' called an underscore and this '_' called a hyphen?	☐	☐

Section B: Punctuation's pertinent

This chapter is a brief reference guide to the grammar, punctuation and other conventions used in the English language and in some of its variants. You can see it's often quite easy to make mistakes – and readers can decode different meanings as a result. So it's very important for you to remember that correct spelling, punctuation and grammar all make your business writing **clear**.

In the following exercise, can you insert any further punctuation that's needed so the message in the letter extract is **clear** and **comprehensible**?

Dear Mrs Smith

This letter is to confirm that your subscription to the following magazine has been cancelled via telephone on 15th November 2012:

Alive and Well (monthly magazine)

We are sorry to see you leave us and would like you to let us know your reasons for terminating the subscription in the feedback form enclosed so that we can improve the quality of our services alternatively you can submit this form online **https://aliveandwellmagazine.com/onlinefeedbackform** on behalf of everyone at alive and Well Magazine as well as Essentials For women publishers we thank you for being a subscriber and hope you return to us again soon yours sincerely

Eliza perry
head Of customer Relations
Essentials for Women Publishers

Chapter Fifteen
The kaleidoscope effect – further perspectives for global business English

> *We all have a voice now. The challenge is knowing when to SHOUT or whisper, when to say something or nothing. But always to listen and learn.*

Mirrors and kaleidoscopes

Congratulations on all you've achieved this far, by being **smart** and **sophisticated**, working through the tips and activities we've given throughout the book. You are sure to be more **confident** in evaluating your communication from many different angles. You can see how you need to adapt the way you project your voice through your writing, and indeed your communication generally.

There are times when you'll need to add or subtract splashes of local colour for **successful**, **clear** and **comprehensible** global business communication in this digital age.

Hold up a figurative mirror to see what reflects back

Knowing that perspectives can so easily diverge, **successful** businesses avoid communication that distorts facts and blurs meanings. They achieve the right focus for the right results.

Aim for that focus by imagining you're holding a mirror. What reflected images do you see regarding the following:

- How do your readers see themselves?

- How do you see yourself as an individual professional – 'brand you' – and as a corporate professional (and as part of a team, if you are)?

- How do you see your readers?

- How might they see you through your writing?

Activity

Jot down your answers here. Your business readers may come from many different sectors and cultures, so you may need to do a number of sub-lists to answer the questions fully.

_____

_____

_____

_____

_____

_____

How did you get on? Just look at your answer to the final question, for example. Was your answer on the lines: 'totally professional'? If so, well done! In fact, did all your answers align the way you think they should? If not, we hope you are now in a position to write down the steps you plan to take to move your career and your business goals to the next level. Now think about the following statement in the box and write down your ideas.

This is what I could do *differently* in order to improve how I see my readers and how they see me:

_____

_____

_____

_____

_____

_____

The global kaleidoscope

Now imagine you're looking through the lens of a kaleidoscope. Imagine that all those splashes of beautiful colour that you see represent the cross-cultural communication of your global audience. By now, you'll understand:

- when to write for the particular elements of the kaleidoscope (most likely using glocal English);
- when to write content that makes the segments drop into place, into one integrated pattern (most likely using global English).

The colours of the kaleidoscope are usually vivid, aren't they? The word power skills you've developed throughout this book should help you write vividly too. It's generally a *must* in this digital age.

Do you remember the sepia-tinted photographs of bygone days? Well old-fashioned, formal writing can seem unintentionally 'sepia-tinted' today, unless you are deliberately using it for an intentionally traditional product. Otherwise 'lacklustre language' is likely to get you noticed (or bypassed) for all the wrong reasons by up-and-coming generations.

Problems other than the English you use

Interestingly, at some point, almost everyone struggles at times to say precisely what they mean to say, even in their native language. Imagine how much more difficult it can be in another language.

Let's loop back now to you and your mother tongue, whatever it is. Again, we stress you need to capture your thoughts correctly in that language, otherwise they are never going to translate well into another. As George Orwell eloquently wrote: 'If people cannot write well, they cannot think well, and if they cannot think well, others will do their thinking for them.'

Sense or nonsense?

To show what we mean, here's an example where the writer of advertising copy in one company (whose native language was English) didn't fully think through how he or she advertised the company's swimwear. The caption beneath a photo of swim shorts made this interesting claim:

> Our swimwear plays harder, dries faster, in or out of the water.

What exactly does this wording mean? The swimwear 'plays'? So is it alive? And how does it 'play harder'? It may dry fast out of water but does it really dry fast in water too? Isn't that impossible? Yet that's the nonsense that the caption claims.

You might ask: Does it matter? It's only swimwear after all: there's no big deal, is there? But there is an important issue here. We don't think the writer necessarily realized that the claims were nonsense. It seems to be a case of flawed logic, as opposed to simply writing zany English copy to grab readers' attention.

And readers notice. Just as they noticed one manufacturer's claim on its printed label on a toy dinosaur: 'realistic sound'. And that's the everyday challenge you face when you write business English. Does it stand up to scrutiny when you're not there to explain it?

You won't get the right results if your starting point is wrong. If the message in your own language isn't right, the best translation in the world can't suddenly produce magical results. That's why so many companies realize that, from time to time, they need to 'go back to the drawing board' and redraft their vision, values or promotional literature in their own language. The word power skills guide in Chapter 8 is of immense value in this respect – it doesn't only apply to English.

Activity

Have you ever seen a message from your organization where, with hindsight, you thought the message hadn't been very well expressed in its original form? If so, can you jot down when this happened? Did you or anyone else follow up on this? If it was not in English, was it subsequently translated into English?

_____

_____

_____

_____

_____

_____

We hope you will look out for this scenario in the future. Vigilance is an excellent way of developing your career and promoting 'brand you'. In fact, have you heard of the fable _'The emperor's new clothes'?_ If so, you'll know that it took one little boy to stand up and say that the emperor's new clothes were not the finest in the world – and that the emperor was actually wearing no clothes at all! There are times when professionals have to stand up too – and question whether a company's writing wears the **smart**, **sophisticated** clothing intended. Is it **clear** and **comprehensible** to all?

Offering or requesting support

Many people dislike having to write in business, even in their own language. Imagine their feelings about having to write in another language, which may be English. It's something to be aware of in a global arena, where you may have to deal with and maybe manage multicultural teams. Training can be a key requirement you need to request or offer.

As writing is a non-negotiable medium, it's a sign of strength, not weakness to question before it's too late. It could cost you time, money and possibly more besides not to get this sort of thing right first time. Be proactive in accessing the right solutions. Here are some more points we can think of to help you write across cultures.

Cultures that are accustomed to say 'yes'

In some cultures, writers will imply 'yes' when they mean 'no'. They may agree to things that are impossible to achieve. They may take on work that is impossible to do. All because their culture doesn't make them feel comfortable saying 'no', they:

- may feel they will appear unprofessional and 'lose face' as a result;
- may believe they will be seen as uneducated and foolish if they do not understand;
- may feel that people will think they lack endurance or resilience (particularly important factors in Asian cultures);
- may prefer to avoid disagreement.

Where you know these are likely reactions, do adapt your writing. You may simply need to ask the right questions to draw out the right answers. For instance, avoid closed questions (ones which typically lead to a 'yes' or 'no' factual answer) and try open questions such as 'why?' or 'how?' The recipient then has to reply in more than one word – and should give a fuller and more informative answer. Here are some examples.

Closed questions

Please can you complete this project by the 31st of this month?
Is the presentation ready?

Open questions

Could you give us an indication as to when you think you could complete this?
What do you think?
How did this happen?
What further information would be useful to you?

Summarizing questions

These are also a useful tool to check that people from different cultures understand the points so far. For example:

So can we confirm: do we all agree that we delay completion of this project for one month?

Cultures that are accustomed to say 'no'

We've just looked at closed questions such as: Please can you let me have this information tomorrow? As we know, some cultures find saying 'no' easy. They may see it as quite all right, indeed supremely efficient, simply to write 'no' in reply to a question. What they may not realize is that they may offend readers from 'yes' or 'maybe' cultures. They won't find the reply 'no' efficient (because they need *reasons why*) and they will also find it rude.

How easily the message could be adapted to suit both cultures, as follows:

I'm afraid I can't get the information to you tomorrow, as it is still being prepared. Will the day after tomorrow be all right for you?

Those in the 'no' culture haven't had to alter their position: they are still not sending the information tomorrow. But there's a shift in tone: they're giving reasons why they are not. In addition they're making some effort to empathize: to check the other person's feelings about this.

Diversity in writing – other challenges

Diversity in writing isn't just about culture. Diversity in learning in the workplace involves other writing challenges, of which dyslexia is one. Sometimes staff will find writing intrinsically difficult. They will need to use different coping strategies – and support – to deliver results.

These are some indicators to look out for, where dyslexic staff may need positive support and encouragement (and the list is by no means exhaustive):

- They may try to keep to the same formats, to keep to constants that they know.
- They may have difficulty remembering language-based information such as instructions or may have difficulty copying from a board.
- They may be embarrassed that you are correcting them – so be sensitive and do not be seen to be picking on them for their dyslexia (which may be undiagnosed).

In Chapter 4 we showed how some fonts will be easier for people with dyslexia and Irlen's syndrome to read, so keep this in mind when you write. Also remember that these people may find having to write in English more difficult than others do.

Using business English to communicate change

Even when you think you have all the answers, something can come along to make you reassess what you do. Yes, you've guessed – a merger or acquisition or some other organizational change. It happens increasingly and you'll need to know how to manage it.

What's more, statistics show that many change initiatives fail, not least because they cause ripples of uncertainty. Staff can feel anxious, even threatened by any change. On top of this, what if they suddenly find they have to use English and they actively don't want to? Or they simply don't feel proficient enough? More than ever, you need to know how to write to allay fears, offer support and set a positive note.

If you're a manager, involve staff in the changes. Encourage everyone to develop strong working relationships, and lead by example. Change may present an opportunity to adopt a new communication style, but it may be best not to be too radical. It can work against you to go overnight from style A to style B, as demonstrated in the following extracts.

Communicating change: Style A

Because of the changes being implemented throughout the company, driven by an identified need to change the existing business model, it is essential that staff acquaint themselves with the new company values and that these are followed strictly at all times.

Communicating change: Style B

Let's welcome this great new start and embrace change wholeheartedly. Let's see work as fun and enjoy growing the company and improving greater profitability for all stakeholders.

Get up to speed with our new values and get on board today!

Such a radical contrast in the two styles may confuse staff and may irritate their cultural sensibilities. They may feel like the 'new outsiders', unable suddenly or easily to relate to the new style. It may even have the undesired effect of making them more resistant to change.

In such instances, consider a transitional style, such as style C, as follows.

Communicating change: Style C

We are all beginning a new journey together. We have a clear vision to take us all forward to new opportunities and growth. We look forward to seizing the opportunity to work with all staff to identify together new values that we can all relate to, as we proceed down this new path to success.

This inclusive style can work well in cross-cultural settings by making staff feel valued, and help them understand change can be good. And the style is relevant to both flat and hierarchical structures. Whatever the cultural demographic, the message is honest and open: *'we're all in this together, so let's get on, work together and enjoy sharing the rewards'*. The essential thing then is to make sure it happens.

Using the right words to motivate

Even native English writers can be surprised at the negative reactions their words can unintentionally stir up. To avoid such reactions, it can help you to categorize in broad terms the sort of words you're likely to write. Here are some examples.

Positive words (that readers generally prefer)

Please   Thank you
Well done   Congratulations
Thanks for your support   I value your input
Thanks for all your efforts/ hard work

Negative words (that readers may rather not see)

No   Can't
Impossible Failure

Relationship-building phrases (that many readers will prefer)

It would greatly assist me/us if you could get these statistics.
I know that it's year end and you are very busy, but may I just ask ....
How is it going?
Do you need any help to meet this tight deadline?
Phrases including people words, for example 'we', 'you'.

Activity

Do any of the words listed above strike a chord with you? Are there any others you can think of? For example, you may have to get some information and get it quickly. You'll need to write words that are likely to help you, and avoid words that will hinder you. Compile a list here, under the three headings given above. It's likely to be of practical assistance to you in the future.

_____

_____

_____

_____

_____

_____

Of course there are times when you have to write negative words to achieve your objectives. If a working environment is hazardous, there are things employees must not do. If you are working where there is a gas leak, you must not light a match. So, to warn people, you could write: *Do not light a match if you suspect a gas leak.* You could make the instruction even more explicit but also actually more helpful, by including the reason why you have to use negative terms: *To avoid the danger of an explosion, if you suspect a gas leak you MUST NOT light a match or any other incendiary device.*

Readers then understand why you write as you do. This can be particularly useful in cross-cultural communication if you have to give instructions. Direct cultures can find that just giving reasons why something needs to be done can make all the difference between success and failure when writing for indirect cultures. By making slight changes, formerly 'harsh' writers found:

- They generally got more assistance.
- They achieved better outcomes.
- Even though nothing about their personalities had changed, they were still viewed in a far more favourable light than previously.

Writing English to lead and motivate just got easier!

Burying good news

If you bury good news in business, you hide positive messages or great results. It often happens when writers get preoccupied with ticking off checklists of things to cover or of points to translate into English.

This next report extract illustrates how one manager got it wrong (from his team's viewpoint) although his intentions were good.

Issues/Concerns

It was a matter of great concern whether the team would be able to function during my naturally unplanned period of one month's sick leave in March, particularly as orders were up 15 per cent on the same period last year.

Our normal contingency plans were in action in case the team found itself unable to deliver but, in the event, they managed to complete on time and within budget.

If we analyse this extract, we see that the extract's heading ('Issues/ Concerns') sounds negative from the outset. Readers expect bad news to follow. Yet what are the key messages here? Are they negative? Far from it, as we find that the division is prospering. Orders were up 15 per cent on the same period last year. The team delivered on time and within budget, even though their manager (the writer) was on sick leave. There's a lot of good news, isn't there?

If writing is to motivate and inspire, don't write headings that unnecessarily fill readers with doom and gloom! If our teams do well (particularly in difficult conditions) then we should be proud of them, shouldn't we? Why not express congratulations?

In the extract that follows, you see how the manager could rewrite the message in a far more positive light, even though all the material facts remain the same.

Congratulations to all staff for excellent results

It was extremely good news for the company that orders were up 15 per cent on the same period last year. The team naturally had to meet extra challenges to deal with this, as I was on sick leave throughout March.

There were the normal contingency plans in action, in case the team needed to draft in extra help in order to deliver. But being the great team they are, they went the extra mile – and completed on time and within budget.

As we've said before, choose with care the headings you write. Chosen well, they plant the right image in your readers' minds. Simply by trading the heading 'Issues/Concerns' for 'Congratulations to all staff for excellent results' readers have the justifiable feel-good factor from the start. This target readership will definitely want to read on.

The improved text then highlights all the positives and very noticeably, introduces the 'people element'. It's no good companies droning on about how people are their most important asset, if they don't then use 'people words' to demonstrate this. It's a simple tip and also one of the most effective you'll find. Once again, we can't stress enough: the world over people buy people. Show this in your writing.

The way forward

Carry on closing the gap from where you were when you began reading this book and where you want to be. You don't want 'brand you' or your organization's brand to stand still, do you? And don't your readers deserve the very best, always? So keep up the activities you have started. Keep developing and adapting your word power skills by using our system in Chapter 8. It works for most every business writing task you're ever likely to undertake.

Remember the kaleidoscope. Remember when to write 'individually coloured pieces' in local or glocal English or when to use global English to pull them all together into a beautiful pattern of understanding.

In a nutshell, taking your business English global involves upholding all the best practice methods you would normally use for a native or local audience, but you also need to reflect diversity, culture and the larger scale of your target global audience in your communications, appropriately and effectively.

There was a beginning to your study, but there should be no end. You have the tips at your disposal to ensure that. Do use them. After all, according to a Chinese proverb, '*Learning is a treasure that will follow its owner everywhere.*'

Happy writing!

Worksheet

Section A: Knowing your theory

Based on what you have understood from this chapter, respond to the following questions and statements by ticking the 'Yes' or 'No' boxes.

	Yes	No
1 Successful business writing is simply about clear meanings.	☐	☐
2 People are always confident when they have to write business English.	☐	☐
3 If your message isn't quite correct in your own language, will it still translate well into another?	☐	☐
4 Is saying 'no' something some cultures avoid?	☐	☐
5 Is it intrusive to provide positive support and coping strategies if staff have writing difficulties?	☐	☐
6 Does organizational change necessitate a swift and radical change in corporate communication style?	☐	☐
7 Is it best to communicate positive news directly?	☐	☐
8 Writing global business English is about balancing the best-practice methods you would use for a native or local audience alongside reflecting diversity, culture and the larger scale of your target global audience.	☐	☐

Section B: Making your business English global

Congratulations on all you have achieved so far! We hope you have enjoyed completing all the worksheets – and leave you with one final exercise to encompass what you have gleaned from this book.

This chapter summarizes the book's key messages. Do glance back over them to refresh your memory from time to time. The main themes are:

- It's best to come over as **smart**, **sophisticated** and **successful** in tone and context.

- It's best to be **clear**, **comprehensible** and **confident** in business writing.

- It's necessary to know when to write global versus glocal business English, with the local splash of colour.

- Use the systematic approach shown in the global word power skills guide, to help you get the right focus, on a daily basis.

Bearing these factors in mind, can you now identify at least seven things you will particularly work on to improve your global business English? Jot them down here, and do revisit this exercise from time to time, as you will find your focus will change as your career progresses and your writing tasks develop.

_____

_____

_____

_____

_____

_____

_____

_____

_____

_____

_____

_____

Chapter Sixteen
Answers to worksheets

Answers to section A questions

Chapter 1

1 Yes
2 Yes
3 Yes
4 Yes
5 Yes
6 No
7 Yes
8 Yes

Chapter 2

1 Yes
2 Yes
3 No
4 Yes
5 Yes
6 No
7 Yes
8 Yes

Chapter 3

1 Yes
2 No
3 Yes
4 No
5 Yes
6 No
7 No
8 Yes

Chapter 4

1 Yes
2 Yes
3 No
4 Yes
5 Yes
6 No
7 Yes
8 Yes

Chapter 5

1 Yes
2 Yes
3 Yes
4 Yes
5 No
6 Yes
7 No
8 No

Chapter 6

1 Yes
2 Yes
3 Yes
4 Yes
5 No
6 Yes
7 No
8 No

Chapter 7

1 Yes
2 No
3 Yes
4 Yes
5 Yes
6 No
7 Yes
8 Yes

Chapter 8

1 Yes
2 Yes
3 No
4 No
5 No
6 Yes
7 Yes
8 Yes

Chapter 9

1 No
2 No
3 Yes
4 Yes
5 Yes
6 Yes
7 Yes
8 No

Chapter 10

1 Yes
2 Yes
3 No
4 No
5 No
6 Yes
7 Yes
8 Yes

Chapter 11

1 No
2 Yes
3 Yes
4 No
5 Yes
6 Yes
7 No
8 Yes

Chapter 12

1 Yes
2 Yes
3 No
4 Yes
5 No
6 Yes
7 No
8 Yes

Chapter 13

1 No
2 Yes
3 Yes
4 Yes
5 No
6 No
7 Yes
8 No

Chapter 14

1 Yes
2 No
3 Yes
4 Yes
5 Yes
6 Yes
7 No
8 No

Chapter 15

1 No
2 No
3 No
4 Yes
5 No
6 No
7 Yes
8 Yes

With over 42 years of publishing, more than 80 million people have succeeded in business with thanks to **Kogan Page**

www.koganpage.com

The sharpest minds need the finest advice. **Kogan Page** creates success.

www.koganpage.com